Headway

Academic Skills

Reading, Writing, and Study Skills

LEVEL 1 **Teacher's Guide**

Richard Harrison
Series Editors: Liz and John Soars

OXFORD

Great Clarendon Street, Oxford, OX2 6DP, United Kingdom

Oxford University Press is a department of the University of Oxford.
It furthers the University's objective of excellence in research, scholarship,
and education by publishing worldwide. Oxford is a registered trade
mark of Oxford University Press in the UK and in certain other countries

First published in 2011

2015 2014 2013

10 9 8 7 6 5

Photocopying

ISBN: 978 0 19 474207 8

Printed in the United Kingdom by Acorn Press Swindon Ltd

This book is printed on paper from certified and well-managed sources

ACKNOWLEDGEMENTS

*The authors and publisher are grateful to those who have given permission to reproduce
the following extracts and adaptations of copyright material:* 8, http://www.
infoplease.com/ce6/world/A0828855.html#ixzz117fbgzRc; 9, http://www.
guardian.co.uk/lifeandstyle/2010/may/10/luisa-dillners-guide-better-memory;
10, BMJ. 2006 October 21; 333(7573): 860. doi: 10.1136/bmj.333.7573.860.

*Although every effort has been made to trace and contact copyright holders before
publication, this has not been possible in some cases. We apologise for any apparent
infringement of copyright and, if notified, the publisher will be pleased to rectify any
errors or omissions at the earliest possible opportunity.*

Contents

Introduction

Headway Academic Skills

A multi-level course aimed at post-secondary students who need English in their academic studies. It comprises a Student's Book and Teacher's Guide for each level.

Each level consists of 10 units covering a variety of topics relevant to students in higher education. Units focus on a wide range of academic reading, writing, research, and/or vocabulary skills.

Headway Academic Skills can be used alongside *New Headway* and *New Headway Plus*, or alongside any other general English course.

Aims of *Headway Academic Skills*

The aims of *Headway Academic Skills* are to help post-secondary students become more efficient and effective in their studies by:

- developing strategies to improve reading speed, and to improve the ability to comprehend complex academic texts;
- developing strategies to produce more coherent writing, and to make clear, appropriate, and relevant notes from academic texts;
- encouraging them to adopt various approaches for dealing with new or unknown vocabulary by practising effective use of dictionaries, and through making effective vocabulary records;
- exploring and evaluating research techniques and resources, and crediting sources of information;
- promoting learner independence by encouraging students to return to earlier Study Skills to refresh their memories, or see how new skills build on and develop those previously presented.

Although the course primarily focuses on the skills of reading, writing, and research, students are given opportunities to practise their listening and speaking skills through brainstorming sessions, discussing issues, and sharing thoughts.

Ultimately, *Headway Academic Skills* also aims to develop academic skills by being transferable to all areas of students' day-to-day academic studies.

What's in the Student's Books?

Each unit consists of 5 × 50–60 minute lessons. There are four or five sections: Reading, Writing, Vocabulary Development and/or Research, and Review. Each Reading, Writing, Vocabulary Development, and Research section has clear study skill aims presented in Study Skill boxes. These skills are practised through a series of controlled to freer practice exercises.

Rules boxes highlight any grammatical areas which students may need as additional support. There is a comprehensive word list at the back of each level.

READING

Each reading section contains one or more texts which students use to develop different study skills. These study skills are clearly detailed in Study Skill boxes and are linked to specific practice exercises. The texts are of various types and styles which students will come across during the course of their academic studies, including scientific reports, articles, biographies, web pages, and data presented through graphics.

WRITING

Each writing section has clear outcomes for the students in terms of the type of text they may be asked to produce in other subjects, including summary writing, a description of a graph, and writing from notes. Skills covered include brainstorming, paragraphing and organizing ideas, linking ideas, and error correction.

VOCABULARY DEVELOPMENT

The vocabulary section contains skills and strategies which help students develop good vocabulary learning and recording techniques. It encourages them to become more autonomous learners by making them more effective users of dictionaries, helping them to work out meanings of new words, and encouraging them to keep coherent and well-organized vocabulary records.

RESEARCH

The principal skills addressed in these sections are formulating efficient search plans, and finding and assessing reliable sources of information such as an encyclopaedia and the Internet. This section also deals with the importance of recording and crediting sources which students use in their academic work.

REVIEW

In the review section, students are given the opportunity to reflect on skills learnt, to practise and develop them further, and to consider how these could be applied to their academic studies.

WORD LISTS

A comprehensive list of words with phonetic transcript from each level of the course can be found in the back of the Student's Book.

Please note that although the level of the vocabulary has been modified to some extent, it reflects the diverse and often more specialized vocabulary found in academic texts. It is not expected that students will learn or indeed need to learn these lists of words.

IELTS and TOEFL

Whilst this course does not deal specifically with the questions which occur in public examinations such as IELTS and TOEFL, many of the skills taught in this course have a direct application to preparing for these exams.

Headway Academic Skills Teacher's Guide

The Teacher's Guide is an easy-to-follow resource for the teacher offering step-by-step guidance to teaching *Headway Academic Skills*. As well as step-by-step procedural notes, the Teacher's Guide contains a summary of aims, lead-in tasks, background information, extension activities, and a comprehensive answer key.

Why use a Teacher's Guide?

Both the Teacher's Guides and the Student's Books have been very carefully devised in order to develop specific academic skills. As such, the treatment of materials is often different from that in a general English course. For example, pre-teaching difficult vocabulary from a text before the students read it may interfere with subsequent skills work on drawing meaning from context, or on extracting only the essential information from a complex text. Teachers are therefore strongly encouraged to consult the Teacher's Guide.

What's in the Teacher's Guide?

AIMS

Each reading, writing, vocabulary development, research, and review section has a summary of the aims of that section.

LEAD IN

Lead-in activities are devised to focus students' attention on the topic and skills of each section.

PROCEDURE

Class management and step-by-step instructions.

BACKGROUND INFORMATION

These notes give teachers background information to the development of a skill, or the topic.

EXTENSION ACTIVITIES

Extension activities offer ideas on how to extend skills practice, or give students an opportunity to reflect on their learning.

ADDITIONAL PHOTOCOPIABLE ACTIVITY

There is one extra practice acivity for each unit with step-by-step instructions at the back of the Teacher's Guide.

ANSWER KEY

For ease of use, the answer key is on the same page as the teaching notes for each exercise, but presented separately. The answer key for each exercise is clearly referenced in the procedural notes. For example, exercise 1 key is referenced ⊙┑1

We hope you and your students enjoy working with Headway Academic Skills.

1 Student life

READING SKILLS Ways of reading
WRITING SKILLS Punctuation (1) • Linking ideas (1) • Checking your writing • Writing about people
VOCABULARY DEVELOPMENT Parts of speech • A dictionary entry (1) • Recording vocabulary (1)

READING How do your read? pp4–5

AIMS

The aim of this section is to get students to think about reading: the reading they do in their studies but also outside their study environment. They will be encouraged to think about the types of texts they have to read and the different skills they use to read each text type.

LEAD IN

• Focus students' attention on the heading *How do you read?* and ask:
  – *What makes a good reader?*
  – *How does a good reader read?*
  – *Are you a good reader? Why?/Why not?*
• Draw students' attention to the picture of the man on page 4 and the woman on page 5. Ask:
  – *Where is the man (woman) and what is he (she) doing?*
  – *Is this a good place to read? Why/Why not?*

PROCEDURE

1 Read the questions quickly with the class. Deal with any vocabulary difficulties. Students complete the quiz individually, then compare their answers with a partner. Go through the questions with the class and discuss their answers. **⊶ 1**

BACKGROUND INFORMATION – READING

Point out the following:
1 It is good to be able to read anywhere, but for study purposes it is best to have a quiet place where you have access to dictionaries, notepaper, pens, etc.
2 The speed of reading depends of what you are reading. Sometimes you do need to read slowly and carefully. Elicit one or two examples from the class (e.g. reading a textbook, understanding instructions).
3 If you check every new word in a dictionary it slows you down. Often you do not need to understand every word, and sometimes you can guess the meaning of a word from the words around it.

2 Read through the words in the box briefly. Give students time to complete the table individually. Check the answers with the class. Point out that the same text can be read in different ways. For example, we read a textbook quickly to find out if it will be useful, or we read it slowly to remember everything. **⊶ 2**

3 Students read the instructions and then read the magazine article. Students compare their answers in pairs. Point out that sometimes we need to read a text slowly and remember it– for example, when learning a poem or definition. **⊶ 3**

4 Students read the instructions and the **Study Skill**. Refer students back to the text in exercise 3. Give students time to complete the exercise. Check the answers with the class. **⊶ 4**

Draw the students' attention to the cartoon. Ask:
– *Where is this woman? What is she trying to do?*

Elicit the answer that she is in a library (or bookshop). She is trying to choose a book quickly (because her son is crying).

EXTENSION ACTIVITY

Ask students to make a list of things they have read in the last week (in any language), including various types of text on the Internet. Then ask them to decide how they read that text – Did they read it quickly or slowly? Did they skim it or scan it? Did they try to remember things? Students compare their answers in pairs, then check answers with the whole class.

READING Answer key pp4–5

⊶ 1
Students' own answers.

⊶ 2
Possible answers
read quickly: newspaper, novel, magazine, telephone directory
read slowly: poem, textbook, report, definition

⊶ 3
Students' own answers.

⊶ 4
1 a study reading
2 c scanning
3 b skimming

WRITING Describing people pp6–7

AIMS

The aim of this section is to help students to write simple paragraphs of description about themselves and other people. It also aims to raise students' awareness of the use of capital letters and the general need for accuracy in writing – the need to check capital letters, spelling, grammar, and punctuation.

LEAD IN

- Write two sentences on the board with no capital letters and no full stop or question mark – for example:
  - *my sister works for the national bank*
  - *how many languages does charles speak*
- Ask:
  - *What is wrong with the sentences?*
  Give the students a few minutes in pairs to discuss the answers.
- Check the suggestions with the class. Elicit the need for capital letters at the beginning of sentences, and for the names of banks and people. Also elicit that punctuation is missing from the sentences – a full stop or question mark is needed at the end of the sentences.
- Ask students:
  - *What other types of word need capital letters?*
  Make a list of suggestions on the board.

PROCEDURE

1 Students read the **Study Skill**. They should compare this list with the list from the lead-in activity.

 Students now read the instructions and match the rules (a–f) with the capital letters in the sentences. Students check their answers in pairs. **⛌ 1**

2 Students read the instructions. Point out that there is more than one sentence in each example. Do the first question together with the class on the board. Students finish the exercise individually. Check the answers with the class. **⛌ 2**

EXTENSION ACTIVITY

Ask students to write one sentence to illustrate each of the rules (a–f). Do the first together as an example. Students write the sentences and then check their sentences with a partner.

3 Students read the instructions. Ask students:
 - *What does 'skim' mean?*

 Check that they understand that it means reading quickly for the general idea. Ask students to look through the two paragraphs quickly to find out what they are about. Elicit general answers, not specific details. **⛌ 3**

4 Read though the table with the class and deal with any difficult vocabulary. Tell students to scan the paragraphs for details about the two people and complete the first two columns of the table with the information. Check answers with the class. **⛌ 4**

5 Students now complete the table with information about themselves. Check to see that students have completed all parts of the table.

6 Refer students to the **Study Skill**. Give students time to study the box.

 Explain the idea that there are many ways of linking sentences. These will be explained in the **Study Skills** on linking ideas throughout the book. Using *and* and *but* are just two examples. Explain that linking the ideas in sentences makes writing easier to read (and more interesting).

 Students now look at the text about Dr Lee again and underline *and* and *but* where they link sentences. **⛌ 6**

 Point out that *but* is usually preceded by a comma. Also point out the fact that not all examples of *and* in the text join sentences, for example: *mathematics and computing*, and *French and Malay*. In these cases *and* is just linking nouns in a list.

WRITING Answer key pp6–7

⛌ 1
1 rule a
2 rule f
3 rule e
4 rule c and rule a
5 rule b
6 rule d

⛌ 2
1 My name is Emin Alpay. I am a teacher at the Middle East Technical University in Ankara.
2 I am a receptionist in a big hotel in Singapore. The name of the hotel is the Royal Palace.
3 My husband is called Sami and he is a pilot. He works for Air New Zealand.
4 Mrs Elly Hollemans is a teacher. She comes from Holland and she teaches German.
5 Where is the Faculty for Oriental Studies? Is it in Oxford?

⛌ 3
Possible answers
The paragraphs describe two different people, their lives, jobs, families, etc.

⛌ 4
Possible answers

	Mona Saeed	Dr Lee
city	Manama	Shanghai, Kuala Lumpur
country	Bahrain	China
job	student	Assistant Professor
age	18	35
flat/house	house	flat
married/single	single	married
children	–	two children
languages	Arabic, English (Farsi)	Chinese, English, French, Malay
other information	likes reading novels, watching TV, playing computer games	likes music, plays the piano, wants to return to China

⛌ 6
Dr Lee is Chinese <u>and</u> comes from Shanghai …
He is a graduate of Shanghai University <u>and</u> has a PhD …
He is 35 years old <u>and</u> he is married …
He likes music very much <u>and</u> he is …
Dr Lee likes teaching at the university, <u>but</u> in the future …

BACKGROUND INFORMATION – LINKING IDEAS

Some of the different ways of making writing more cohesive have been collected under the heading 'Linking ideas'. This heading is used in different **Study Skills** throughout the book. They include the use of conjunctions (*and, but, so*), sentence connectors (*first, however, in addition*), relative pronouns (*which, that, where*) and subordinators (*because*).

7 Students work individually and join the pairs of sentences. Check answers with the class. 🔑 7

8 Students read the instructions and the RULES box. Ask students to look at the paragraph about Mona again and notice the Present Simple verbs, e.g. *is, am, is, am, hope, am, am, have, live, speak* (they could underline them). Students then write a similar paragraph about themselves. Final drafts of the paragraphs (corrected versions – see exercises 10 and 11) could later be collected and displayed.

Writing about people p7

9 Ask students to look at the paragraph about Dr Lee. Point out the Present Simple verbs – *is, comes, teaches*, etc.

Ask students to draw a table like the one on page 7 (city, country, job, etc) in their notebooks, with one column for information. Put students into pairs and tell them to interview one another and collect information to put in the table. Students then write a paragraph about their partner. 🔑 9

10 Students read the instructions and the **Study Skill**. They then correct the mistakes in the sentences. Check answers with the class. 🔑 10

11 Students read the instructions, then check and correct their own paragraphs.

EXTENSION ACTIVITY

Ask students to draw another table in their notebooks. They should then find another person to interview outside the classroom – a teacher, a friend, a relative, etc. They then write a paragraph about this person. Students could read their (corrected) paragraphs to the class, or they could be part of a class display.

ADDITIONAL PHOTOCOPIABLE ACTIVITY

Writing 1 Punctuation

VOCABULARY DEVELOPMENT
Dictionary work (1) p8

AIMS

One aim of this section is to make sure that students are familiar with the basic parts of speech. The section also aims to encourage students to explore their dictionaries. It shows them that a dictionary does not only give the meanings of words, but also provides other useful information.

In addition, this section gets students to think about ways of organizing and recording vocabulary that they want to learn.

LEAD IN

- Put students into pairs or small groups.
- Ask them to make a list of all the things we can find out about a word by looking in a dictionary.
- Collect ideas from the whole class and make a list on the board.
- Add any points they may have missed (e.g. parts of speech, pronunciation, plural forms, the forms of a verb, examples of use, opposites).
- Check that students are familiar with the term *parts of speech*. Write two sentences on the board, e.g.
  – *George is in the <u>office</u> at the moment.*
  – *George <u>studies</u> French and mathematics.*
- Point to each underlined word and ask:
  – *What part of speech is this?*
  Elicit the answers (*office* is a noun and *studies* is a verb).

🔑 7

1 I am 18 years old and I am single.
2 I am from Turkey and I live in the capital, Ankara.
3 Joe comes from India, but he is working in Germany at the moment.
4 Maria and Jose are married and they have four children.
5 Sam likes computers, but he doesn't like computer games.
6 I want to build a big villa near my parents' house, but I have no money.

🔑 9

Students' own answers, but the texts in exercise 3 are a model.

🔑 10

My nam<u>e</u> is Sonia. I come from <u>B</u>razil. I am <u>a</u> teacher in a school<u>.</u> My husband work<u>s</u> in <u>a</u> bank. His name is <u>R</u>iccardo. We have two <u>children</u>.

PROCEDURE

1 Students read the **Study Skill** on parts of speech. Make sure they are familiar with the main parts of speech. Give further examples if necessary, using full sentences as in the lead in. For example:
  – *Physics is a <u>difficult</u> subject for many students.* (adjective)
  – *Karen did <u>badly</u> in the final exam.* (adverb)
  – *The mobile was <u>under</u> the newspaper.* (preposition)
Students complete exercise 1, then check answers with the class. 🔑 1

EXTENSION ACTIVITY

Ask students to work in pairs. Ask them to give two examples for each of the parts of speech mentioned in the **Study Skill**. Check all the words. Students then write the words in full sentences.

2 Ask students to read the **Study Skill**. Check the list with the list that the class came up with in the lead in.

Students then look at the extracts from the *Oxford Essential English Dictionary*. Ask students to find the dictionary entry for the word *suburb*. Point out the information on pronunciation, part of speech, and meaning, and also the example sentence. Refer to the information for *suburb* in the table.

Students now work individually and complete the table with information on the other three words. Check answers with the class. 🔑 2

3 Students read the **Study Skill** and the instructions. Point out that it is easier to learn and remember vocabulary if it is in groups. Students complete the lists in pairs and add any other words they know. Check answers with the class. 🔑 3

EXTENSION ACTIVITY

Ask students to work in pairs to think of three other groups for organizing vocabulary (e.g. electrical appliances, fruit, feelings). They should give at least three or four words for each group. Get some pairs to read out their lists to the rest of the class.

REVIEW p9

AIMS

The aim of this section is to encourage students to review the content of the unit and also to practise and develop the skills they have learnt.

PROCEDURE

1 Students read the instructions, then allow students time to read the questions. Explain any vocabulary students do not understand. Refer students back to the **Study Skill** on parts of speech and a dictionary entry to help them answer the questions. Students answer the questions individually or in pairs. Check answers with the class. 🔑 1

2 Elicit from the class the rules about using capital letters. Then tell students to read the **Study Skill** on page 6. Students then complete the exercise. 🔑 2

3 Refer students back to the **Study Skill** on recording vocabulary on page 8. Get students to complete the task and add other words they know. Check answers with the whole class. 🔑 3

4 Students read the instructions. Students then find three (or more) new words in the unit and complete the table. 🔑 4

VOCABULARY DEVELOPMENT Answer key p8

🔑 1

1 lives – verb
2 parents – noun
3 in – preposition
4 of – preposition
5 usually – adverb
6 read – verb
7 carefully – adverb
8 interesting – adjective
9 language – noun
10 difficult – adjective

🔑 2

Possible answers

quick /kwɪk/, adjective, taking little time/fast: *It's quicker to travel by plane than by train.*

check /tʃek/, verb, to look at something to see that it is right, good or safe: *Do the sums and then use a calculator to check your answers.*

always /ˈɔːlweɪz/, adverb, at all times, every time: *I have always lived in London.*

🔑 3

jobs: translator, builder, accountant, pilot, doctor, teacher, professor
family: sister, father, mother, cousin, brother, aunt, uncle
homes: house, flat, apartment, villa, hostel, palace

REVIEW Answer key p9

🔑 1

1 adverb
2 one
3 truck
4 easy
5 /mæɡəˈziːnz/
6 bought
7 addresses
8 mathematical
9 a poet
10 down

🔑 2

1 My friend Igor comes from Moscow.
2 I am studying French and history at Manchester University.
3 Is Charles doing a course at Capital Institute?
4 My brother wants to visit Turkey and Germany next summer.
5 Is there a message from Mr Hector Ortiz from Mexico?
6 The name of the hotel is Al Bustan Palace. It is just outside Riyadh.

🔑 3

Possible answers

Things we read: novel, poem, dictionary, newspaper, textbook, magazine, report, telephone directory, book

Academic subjects: physics, English, French, Russian, computer programming, mathematics, history, science

🔑 4

Students' own answers.

2 Daily routines

READING SKILLS Predicting content (1) • Skimming
WRITING SKILLS Handwriting • Paragraphs • Linking ideas (2) • Writing about routine and procedure
VOCABULARY DEVELOPMENT Collocations • Jobs ending in -er, -or, -ist

READING Work and stress pp10–11

AIMS

This section introduces the idea of making predictions about the content of a text before reading it, as an aid to comprehension. In particular, it focuses on the skill of looking at the pictures in a text to predict meaning. It also aims to give further practice in the skill of skimming a text for the general idea.

LEAD IN

- Write three jobs on the board, for example: *gardener, pilot, bank clerk*
- Ask students to work in pairs and to think about the good points (advantages) and bad points (disadvantages) of each job.
- Discuss the ideas briefly with the class. Try to elicit the words *healthy*, *salary*, and *stress* in the discussion.

PROCEDURE

1 Introduce this activity as a mini-survey. Tell students to read the instructions and to look at the table. Working with a partner, they should then complete the table. Point out that they can write any combination of numbers – for example, 1, 1, 1 if they think that all factors are very important. Collect the results for the whole class. Make totals for each factor and display them in a table on the board, e.g. a) 21, b) 32, c) 19. Use the results for a discussion on the relative importance of these three factors.

2 Tell students to read the **Study Skill**, and make sure they understand the word *predict*.

   Read the instructions and the example sentence with the class. Students then identify the jobs of the other people and make similar sentences about them. They then discuss in pairs whether the jobs are healthy or stressful, and give their reasons. Discuss the answers with the class. ⊶ 2

3 Elicit the difference between skimming and scanning. Tell students to read the **Study Skill** to check that they remember correctly. Students read the instructions, then skim the article quickly to choose headings for each paragraph. Students check their answers in pairs. ⊶ 3

4 Students read the article to check their predictions from exercise 2.

5 Ask students to read the instructions, then ask them to say what a summary is. Elicit these facts:
   – it is shorter than the original text   – it contains the main points
   – it is useful for revision later on

   Students complete the summary individually using the words in the box. Check answers with the class. ⊶ 5

EXTENSION ACTIVITY

1 Tell students to go back and re-read the text *How do you read?* on page 5. Tell them to find the main points of the text and write two or three sentences to summarize the text.

2 Get students to bring in texts which have accompanying pictures, or bring in a set of your own. Get students to work in pairs. Give each pair a text and ask: *What do you think the texts are about?*

   They should look at the pictures and make predictions about each text. If the texts are not too difficult, encourage them to skim the text to see if their predictions were correct.

READING Answer key pp10–11

⊶ 2

Possible answers

A florist sells flowers. A taxi driver drives people from one place to another for money. A fireman puts out fires. A personal trainer helps people to keep fit/lose weight.

A florist and a personal trainer are not stressful jobs. A taxi driver and a fireman are stressful.

⊶ 3

1 Jobs that are healthy
2 Stressful jobs
3 What people want

⊶ 5

Some jobs, for example, **a florist**, a personal trainer, and a nutritionist, are **healthy**. These jobs have very little **stress** or worry. Other jobs, however, are very **unhealthy**. An example is a taxi driver. He **drives** people all day and often faces **traffic** problems. It is difficult to get a job that is **interesting** and healthy and also has a good **salary**.

WRITING Routines and procedures pp12-13

AIMS

The aim of this section is to get students to think about the presentation of their written work, in particular, handwriting and paragraphing.

This section also focuses on routines and procedures. It helps students to understand the structure of texts which describe a routine (e.g. a daily routine) or a procedure (e.g. writing an academic essay). Students are then guided towards writing their own descriptions of routines and procedures.

LEAD IN

- Write the word *routine* on the board and elicit examples of routines, e.g. a work routine or a school routine. Ask some students to describe their daily routine.
- Then write the word *procedure* on the board.
- Elicit that a procedure is a way of doing a particular task, and elicit examples, e.g. registering for a course, sending an email, opening a bank account, etc.
- Choose one procedure, e.g registering for a course, and elicit the steps in the procedure (e.g. look at the list of courses, discuss the options with a tutor, choose a course, etc.).

PROCEDURE

1 Ask students:

 – *When do you need to write by hand?*

Make a list on the board with the class. Then ask students to read the **Study Skill** on handwriting. Ask the class to compare the list in the book with their suggestions. Discuss any additional occasions when handwriting is important.

Students then read the instructions individually and match the mistakes with the examples (a–f) in the paragraph. Check answers with the class and elicit from students their own problems with handwriting. **⚬┐1**

2 Ask students:

 – *What is a paragraph?*
 – *How do we show when a new paragraph begins?*

Listen to the students' answers and then direct them to the **Study Skill** on paragraphs. Give them time to read the information and make sure they have understood everything.

Students now read the instructions for the exercise and look at the text about Helena. Students discuss their answers in pairs, then check answers with the class. **⚬┐2**

3 Students write out the text as two paragraphs, using either block or indented styles. Make sure they leave double spacing between paragraphs if using the block style. Check that the indentations are the same length if they use the indented style. **⚬┐3**

4 Students read the **Study Skill**. Elicit other examples of sequencing words (e.g. *secondly, next, lastly*) and time expressions (*in the evening, last week, in March*).

Students then read the instructions and complete the exercise. Check answers with the class. **⚬┐4**

5 Ask students to point out the time expressions in the text (*at 11 o'clock, at about 1 o'clock, in the afternoon*). Tell them they can use these time expressions as well as the sequencing words to help them put the sentences in order. Students complete the task individually, then check their answers in pairs. **⚬┐5**

EXTENSION ACTIVITY

Ask students to write out the two paragraphs correctly. Tell them to use either indented or block style.

6 Write on the board the title: *How to Plan and Write an Essay*. Elicit ideas from students and write down the steps they come up with. Then draw their attention to the instructions. Get them to look at the words in the box and the paragraph about Maria. Students complete the paragraph.

Discuss briefly the steps Maria uses to write an essay. Compare them with the steps the class mentioned earlier. **⚬┐6**

WRITING Answer key pp12-13

⚬┐1

a3 b2 c1 d5 e6 f4

⚬┐2

1 There is a mixture of styles – some paragraphs are indented and some are block style.
2 Some paragraphs have fewer than three sentences.

⚬┐3

Two paragraphs, either block or indented style.
Paragraph 1 begins: "My sister, Helena is …"
Paragraph 2 begins: "At the weekends …"

⚬┐4

Then First After that Finally After (the class)

⚬┐5

Paragraph 1
1 Maria usually gets to the university at about 8.30.
2 First, she has a cup of tea in the snack bar.
3 Then she goes to her first class. This is at 9 o'clock.
4 At 11 o'clock she has another class. This is poetry.
5 After that, she goes to the library and studies for an hour before lunch.

Paragraph 2
6 At about 1 o'clock Maria goes to the student canteen with some of her friends.
7 They talk about their studies or their plans for the weekend.
8 In the afternoon Maria has one more class from 2 o'clock to 3.30.
9 After the class she goes to the library again for another hour.
10 Finally, she leaves the university at about 5. It is a long day.

⚬┐6

1 First
2 Next
3 while
4 After
5 Then
6 Finally

Writing about routine and procedure p13

7 Put students into pairs and tell them they are going to write about their partner's daily routine.

First, they should interview their partner and take notes.

Help them to start the interview by getting suggestions for questions:
– *When do you leave home?*
– *When do you get to the university/school?*
– *What do you do first?*
– *What do you do after that?* etc.

When students have finished taking notes, explain that they are going to write two paragraphs so they should decide which information will go in each paragraph (e.g. morning routine, afternoon routine). Refer them back to the paragraphs about Maria's daily routine in exercise 4. Tell them they can use these paragraphs as a model for their own.

Remind them that they should use suitable sequencing words and time expressions. Refer them to the ideas in the box, and also the words and expressions used in exercises 4 and 6.

Remind students to check their writing carefully. They should check spelling, capital letters, punctuation, grammar, and paragraphing. If they are writing by hand, remind them of the rules for good handwriting.

Students write their paragraphs. **⊙—7**

8 Read the instruction with the class and elicit ideas from the class on how they revise for exams.

Read through the ideas in the box with the class and explain any difficult vocabulary. Then ask students to write the paragraph, using sequencing words and time expressions. Remind them again to check their writing at the end.
⊙—8

EXTENSION ACTIVITY

Ask students to think again about the way they plan formal writing – a letter, a project, a report, etc. (not necessarily in English). Get them to write down the steps they follow. They should then write a paragraph outlining the steps in their writing process.

ADDITIONAL PHOTOCOPIABLE ACTIVITY

Writing 2 Sequencing

VOCABULARY DEVELOPMENT
Words that go together p14

AIMS

The aim of this section is to introduce the idea of collocation as a useful tool for vocabulary building. The section also focuses on the organization of words related to jobs, and spelling rules for the different word endings.

LEAD IN

- Write a sentence on the board with a missing verb, for example:
  – *Paulo has to … an essay on climate change this evening.*
- Ask students to think of verbs which can go in the space (*write, plan, read*, etc.) and point out that certain words collocate (go with) with each other. Give some other examples of nouns and elicit the verbs that collocate with them, e.g.
  – *play + football*
  – *watch + television*
- Write a second sentence:
  – *I have got two … tickets in my case.*
- Elicit possible answers (*plane, train, bus* etc.) and point out that nouns can also collocate with other nouns.

PROCEDURE

1 Tell students to read the **Study Skill** on collocations. Check that they understand the word *collocation* and also the verb *collocate*.

Students then complete the diagrams for the words *traffic* and *have*. Students

⊙—7

Students' own answers, but the paragraphs in exercise 4 are models.

⊙—8

Students' own answers, but the paragraph in exercise 6 is a model.

VOCABULARY DEVELOPMENT Answer key p14

⊙—1a

Possible answers
traffic: jam, warden, lights, police, accident
have: breakfast, lunch, dinner, a shower, a bath, a meeting, a lecture, an interview

⊙—1b

1e 2f 3d 4c 5g 6a 7b

can use dictionaries to help them if necessary. ⊙━ 1a

Students then read the instructions for the activity and match the verbs with the nouns individually. Check answers with the class. ⊙━ 1b

2 Tell students to use their dictionaries for this exercise. They should look up the underlined words (for example, *walk*) to find which verbs collocate with it. Do the first with the class as an example and let students complete the exercise on their own. ⊙━ 2

3 Students use their dictionaries to find other nouns which collocate with the nouns *computer* and *business*. Check answers with the class. ⊙━ 3

Spelling (1) p14

4 Students read the instructions and the RULES box. They then complete the definitions of the six jobs, using dictionaries to check the spellings. ⊙━ 4

5 Students work in pairs to write the jobs from exercise 4 in the table, and add ideas of their own. ⊙━ 5

REVIEW

AIMS

The aim of this section is to encourage students to review the content of the unit and also to practise and develop the skills they have learnt.

PROCEDURE

1 Students read the instructions and the example answers. They then look back through the unit and choose five other jobs from the unit and write similar sentences. Students check their sentences in pairs. ⊙━ 1

2 Refer students back to the **Study Skill** on page 13.

Students then read the instructions to this exercise and the sentences in the box. Tell students to read quickly through the text on Sam's day before they complete it with the missing sentences. Students complete the paragraph individually, using the sentences from the box. Check answers with the class. ⊙━ 2a

EXTENSION ACTIVITY

Ask students to look at the paragraph about Sam. Remind them of the rule for paragraphing (page 12). Ask them to divide the paragraph into three possible paragraphs. Check their solution and ask them to write out the three paragraphs. ⊙━ 2b

3 Read the instructions with the class. Students work individually, then compare their answers in pairs. They then write their paragraphs individually. Remind students to use sequencing words in their paragraph.

4 Refer students back to the **Study Skill** on page 14. Students then read the instructions and look at tables A and B. Point out the examples that are given. Students then complete table A with at least one noun for each verb, and table B with at least one verb for each noun. Tell students to use their dictionary where necessary. Check answers with the class. ⊙━ 4

⊙━ 2

1 went for
2 had
3 tell
4 catches/takes/gets
5 lose
6 take/get

⊙━ 3

Possible answers
computer: virus, program, programmer, programming, training, games, hacker, software
business: studies, administration, management, trip, -man, -woman, plan, meeting, lunch

⊙━ 4

1 scientist
2 doctor
3 shopkeeper
4 florist
5 actor
6 interpreter

⊙━ 5

-er: taxi driver, interpreter, shopkeeper + builder, teacher, manager, etc.
-or: professor, doctor, actor + translator, refuse collector, etc.
-ist: journalist, scientist, florist + receptionist, chemist, etc.

REVIEW Answer key p15

⊙━ 1

Possible answers
A professor teaches in a university.
A journalist writes articles for a newspaper.
A nutritionist tells people what food they should eat to stay healthy.

⊙━ 2a

1 First he has a quick breakfast in the hotel coffee shop.
2 Then he goes to his office.
3 Next, he speaks to the hotel staff.
4 After that, he has a meeting with his manager.
5 In the afternoon, he goes back to his office.
6 Finally, at about 4 o'clock Sam leaves work.

⊙━ 2b

Paragraph 1: Sam is the assistant manager …
Paragraph 2: First, he has a quick breakfast …
Paragraph 3: In the afternoon, he goes …

⊙━ 4

Possible answers
A
face: the front, the garden
train: people, horses
scan: an article, a list
spend: time, money
B
send, receive, get   emails
make, receive, get   telephone calls
have, attend   a meeting
start up, turn off   the computer

READING SKILLS Scanning – using headings • Meaning from context
WRITING SKILLS Punctuation (2) • Talking about frequency • Writing about study habits
RESEARCH Sources
VOCABULARY DEVELOPMENT Recording vocabulary (2)

READING Weather pp16–17

AIMS

The aim of this section is to encourage students to get information quickly from a text, in particular from an encyclopaedia entry, by learning to use headings. It also encourages students to make their reading more efficient by developing the skill of guessing the meaning of a word from its context.

LEAD IN

- Ask students:
  – *What are the seasons of the year?*
  Write them on the board.
- Ask:
  – *What is your favourite season and why?*
- Get students to work in pairs. Ask them to write weather vocabulary associated with each season (e.g. *summer – hot, dry, sunny*).
- Collect the vocabulary from the class. Add words to the board in a spidergram for each season.
- Write the word *hurricane* on the board. Elicit the meaning, and ask students what they know about hurricanes. Ask where they could go to find out more information.
- Elicit the word *encyclopaedia*. Point out that some encyclopaedias are available online (e.g. Wikipedia).

PROCEDURE

1 Refer students to the pictures and the titles. Students match the titles with the pictures. **○━1**

2 Students match the words with the pictures. Point out that some words could be used for more than one picture. Check answers and explain any vocabulary that students do not understand. **○━2**

3 Put students into pairs. Ask them to use the words in exercise 2 to discuss the weather in the pictures. Give them some questions to ask, e.g.:
  – *What is the weather like in picture …?*
  – *What country is this?*
  – *Do you think it is warm, or cold?* **○━3**

4 Read the questions quickly with the class and deal with any vocabulary difficulties. Students work in pairs and try to answer the questions. Listen to the students' answers quickly, but do not say if they are right or wrong at this stage.

5 Check that students remember the meaning of scanning – reading quickly to find information.

  Tell students to read the **Study Skill** on scanning and using headings.

  Students then read the text to check their answers from exercise 4. Do the first with the class as an example. Show them how to use the heading *Naming hurricanes* to quickly find the answer (Yes).

  Students use the headings in a similar way to check the answers for questions 2–5. **○━5**

6 To introduce the idea of context, write this sentence on the board:
  – *In the very cold winter months the river <u>freezes</u> over and it is possible to walk on the ice.*

  Ask:
  – *What part of speech is 'freezes'?* (a verb)

READING Answer key pp16–17

○━1

1 b Desert morning
2 c A winter's day
3 a Hurricane season

○━2

Possible answers
a heavy rain, strong winds, wet, warm, storm
b dry, blue sky, hot, sunny
c snow, cold, ice

○━3

Students' own answers.

○━5

1 Yes
2 Hurricanes are found in the Atlantic Ocean, the Caribbean Sea and the Gulf of Mexico. They are called typhoons in the Pacific Ocean.
3 We measure them by categories, from 1–5.
4 The eye
5 In the Atlantic, in summer and autumn. In the north-west Pacific, all the year round.

Elicit that if we don't know the meaning of the word *freezes* we can use the words around it (*cold, winter, river, walk on*) to guess the meaning (change from liquid to solid because of the cold).

Students now read the **Study Skill** and answer the questions (*rotate* is a verb, and it means 'move in a circle').

Students now read the instructions and complete the table with the part of speech and the correct meaning from the box. Check answers with the class. 🔑 **6**

WRITING Describing our lives pp18–19

AIMS
This section teaches students to write paragraphs describing routines (for example, how they spend their summer) or habits (for example, study habits). It encourages them to use frequency adverbs correctly in their writing. This section also aims to clarify the use of the apostrophe for possession and in contractions.

LEAD IN
- Write two example sentences on the board to show the two different uses of apostrophes. For example:
  – *Mary's sick today.*
  – *Mary's essay was excellent.*
- Elicit the word *apostrophe* and elicit that in the first sentence it is used for a contraction, and in the second sentence it shows possession.
- Point out that contractions should be avoided in formal or academic writing.

PROCEDURE
1 Students read the **Study Skill** on apostrophes. Make sure students understand the difference between *boy's computer* (one boy) and *the boys' computer* (more than one boy). Students read the instructions and complete the exercise. 🔑 **1**

2 Students read the instructions and the sentences. Point out that not all the sentences require apostrophes. The first sentence could be done with the class as an example. Students then complete the task individually and check their answers in pairs. 🔑 **2**

3 Tell students to read the text on deserts quickly. Point out that the text uses contractions and elicit that this is a formal essay and so should not use contractions.

Read the task with the class and point out that one has been done for them. Students complete the task individually. Check the answers with the class.

Point out that there are two examples of possession in the text (*Earth's, world's*). Students should not change these. 🔑 **3**

4 Refer students to the picture and elicit that it is a holiday home. Ask students:
– *How do you usually spend your summer holidays?*

Encourage students to use *usually, never, always,* etc. with their answers, e.g.:
– *I usually go on holiday with my family.*

Explain that words like *usually* and *sometimes* are adverbs of frequency.

Students then read the instructions and circle the adverbs of frequency in the text. Check answers with the class. 🔑 **4a**

Ask about the position of *sometimes* and elicit that it occurs in two positions – before the verb and the beginning of the sentences.

Students then read the RULES box and complete the rules and the ranking of the five adverbs. Check answers with the class. 🔑 **4b**

5 Read the task with the class. Read through the ideas in the box with the class and elicit other ideas they may want to include in their paragraphs (e.g. read books, travel abroad, go shopping). Write these on the board.

Students then write a paragraph about their summer. Remind them to use adverbs of frequency. 🔑 **5**

6 Refer students to the questionnaire and elicit that a questionnaire is one way of collecting information or data. It consists of a list of questions.

Look at the study habits questionnaire with the class and elicit that your study habits are the ways in which you usually study. Ask students to put the words in the right order to make questions. 🔑 **6**

🔑 **6**
1 huge: *adjective*, very big
2 occasionally: *adverb*, sometimes
3 track: *verb*, follow
4 continues: *verb*, goes on
5 peak: *noun*, the high point
6 region: *noun*, part of the world

WRITING Answer key pp18–19

🔑 **1**
1 contraction (Nori has got …)
2 possession (The car belonging to Nori.)
3 contraction (Nori is …)
4 possession (The telephone number belonging to Nori.)

🔑 **2**
1 Have you got the girl's books? She's looking for them.
2 My favourite seasons are spring and summer. The weather's beautiful then.
3 The students' exam results were very bad. They all have to retake them.
4 Don't swim today. The waves are huge and they're very dangerous!
5 In the winter months many students go skiing in the mountains. (No change)
6 A Where's Mike's computer?
   B I've got it here.

🔑 **3**
rainfall's = rainfall is
there's = there is
don't = do not
They're = They are
can't = can not (cannot)
doesn't = does not.

🔑 **4a**
we **always** go …,
The weather is **usually** warm …
it **sometimes** rains …
My brothers like swimming and they **often** go there.
The water is **always** freezing …
I **never** swim.
Sometimes the whole family goes for a walk …
I do not **usually** cook …

🔑 **4b**
a **after** the main verb
b **before** the main verb

ranking: always, usually, often, sometimes, never

🔑 **5**
Students' own answers, but the text in exercise 4 is a model.

🔑 **6**
1 Where do you like to study?
2 When do you usually study?
3 How do you prefer to study?
4 Do you make notes when you study?
5 How many hours do you study in a week?
6 How often do you make a study plan?

7 Students read the text and circle the answers to complete the questionnaire for Suresh. Check answers with the class. **O─ 7**

8 Students go through the questionnaire again. This time they give answers in their notebooks about their own study habits. Make sure they give a reason for each answer. **O─ 8**

9 Put students into pairs. They now interview each other and ask about their study habits. They should use the questions from the questionnaire and make a note of the reasons their partners give. Encourage students to discuss how their study habits are different.

Get a few of the pairs to tell the class about their results. **O─ 9**

10 Read through the **Study Skill** with the class and point out that everyone studies in their own way, but these are useful tips. Ask students if they can add to the list.

Look at the example of a study plan with the students. Tell them they are going to design their own study plan. First, plan the grid with the class. Get students to write in their class/lecture hours. Then ask them to think about their study hours and add them to the grid. Get students to exchange their plans and talk about them with a partner. **O─ 10**

Writing about study habits p19

11 Read the instructions with the class. Tell students to read the paragraph about Suresh again, and tell them they can use that as a model for their own writing. Students write a paragraph about their own study habits, using the notes they made. Remind them to use some adverbs of frequency, and to check their writing carefully when they have finished. **O─ 11**

EXTENSION ACTIVITY

Ask students to write a similar paragraph about their partner. They should use the notes they made.

ADDITIONAL PHOTOCOPIABLE ACTIVITY

Writing 3 Pronouns and the words they refer to

RESEARCH Finding information (1) p20

AIMS

The aim of this section is to get students to think about the various sources of information they can use for their studies. It aims to show that there are many different sources and that the Internet is only one of them.

LEAD IN

- Write a question on the board that requires a factual answer, for example:
  – *What is the capital city of Papua New Guinea?*
- Elicit various ways in which students could find this information, including an atlas, encyclopaedia, books, and the Internet.
- Write the expression *source of information* on the board and explain that encyclopaedias, books, and the Internet are all sources of information.

PROCEDURE

1 Students read the **Study Skill**. Point out that a source of information should be reliable and also up-to-date. Point out that students should always make a note of the sources they use.

Students then read the instructions and complete the diagram. Students check their answers in pairs. Then draw the diagram on the board and invite answers from the class to complete the diagram. **O─ 1**

2 Students read the instructions. Read through the questions with the class and deal with any vocabulary difficulties. Students decide what sources they will use. **O─ 2**

3 Students complete this task outside of the classroom. Check their answers later in the class. Discuss the sources with the students. Carry out a quick survey in the class to find the answer to question 9. **O─ 3**

O─ 7

1b 2b 3a 4a 5c 6c

O─ 8

Students' own answers.

O─ 9

Students' own answers.

O─ 10

Students' own answers.

O─ 11

Students' own answers, but the paragraph in exercise 7 is a model.

RESEARCH Answer key p20

O─ 1

Possible answers
Internet, encyclopaedia, textbooks, journals, magazines, reports, newspapers, interviews (people), questionnaires, experiments, observation, TV/radio programmes, atlas/maps

O─ 2

Possible answers
1 dictionary
2 Internet
3 encyclopaedia
4 atlas
5 newspaper/radio
6 physics textbook
7 cookbook/encylopaedia
8 biography/history textbook
9 survey/questionnaire

O─ 3

Possible answers
1 search (*verb*): to look carefully because you are trying to find somebody or something
2 –
3 1324 BC
4 India and China
5 –
6 *'Each object in the universe attracts each other body'* Newton's Law of Gravity
7 pasta, made from flour and water, was made famous in Italy (though first made in China as 'noodles')
8 Porbandar, Gujurat, India
9 –

EXTENSION ACTIVITY

In groups, students design their own quiz along the lines of the questions on page 20. Groups then exchange the quiz with another group. The group completes the quiz as before. Finally, results are checked in the class.

VOCABULARY DEVELOPMENT
Drawing and diagrams   p20

AIMS
The aim of this section is to introduce another technique for learning vocabulary – by using drawings and diagrams.

LEAD IN
- Refer students back to the **Study Skill** on recording vocabulary (page 8). Elicit that it suggests organizing words into groups.
- Write the word *wind* on the board and check the meaning.
- Ask students to draw a picture to help them remember the word. Get students to show their pictures.
- Now write the words *warm, cold, cool,* and *hot* on the board. Nearby draw a vertical arrow. Ask students to arrange the words in order.
- Explain that these are other ways of recording vocabulary.

1 Students read the **Study Skill** on the use of pictures and ranking to record vocabulary.

Students read the instructions, then look up the meanings of the words and make drawings.

Point out the two examples of grading in the box. Give students another example to reorder, e.g. *large, small, extra-large, medium.*

REVIEW   p21

AIMS
The aim of this section is to encourage students to review the content of the unit and also to practise and develop the skills they have learnt.

PROCEDURE

1 Ask students to look through the Reading section of the unit and to write down vocabulary to do with the weather. Revise parts of speech by writing three sentences on the board to illustrate noun, adjective, and verb. For example:
– *There is a lot of <u>rain</u> in the winter.* (noun)
– *It is very <u>windy</u> today.* (adjective)
– *It is very cold. I think it will <u>snow</u> later.* (verb)

Ask them to identify the parts of speech. They should then read the instructions and complete the table, using dictionaries as necessary. **1**

2 Point out the visuals on page 21. Students read the task and draw their own visuals. Get them to compare with other students. Choose a few students to draw their examples on the board. **2**

3 Refer students back to the RULES box on adverbs of frequency (page 18). Remind them of the position of the adverbs of frequency in relation to the verb.

Students reorder the words to make sentences. Check the answers with the class. **3**

4 Students rewrite the sentences with the adverbs of frequency. Point out that there are two possible answers for number 6. **4**

5 Ask students to complete the five sentences with the five verbs. Remind them that some nouns collocate with certain verbs (**Study Skill** page 14). **5**

1

snow – snowy – to snow
wind – windy
ice – icy – to ice over
rain – rainy – to rain
cloud – cloudy – to cloud over
sun – sunny
warmth – warm – to warm (up)
heat – hot – to heat
fog – foggy

2

Students' own answers.

3

1 Hurricanes usually form in the summer months.
2 Tony never studies at the weekend.
3 Deserts are sometimes cold at night. (Sometimes deserts are cold at night.)
4 I don't very often go to the cinema.
5 The weather is always beautiful in India in September. (or, In September the weather …)

4

1 Maureen usually likes studying at night.
2 Why is Yuki always late for work?
3 It never rains in the summer where I live.
4 I often read the newspaper.
5 The winters are usually long and cold in my country.
6 Kim sometimes stays at home at weekends. (Sometimes Kim stays at home at weekends.)

5

1 look up
2 surf
3 consult
4 interview
5 read

4 Architecture

READING SKILLS Making notes (1)
RESEARCH Focusing your search
WRITING SKILLS Linking ideas (3) and (4) • Words and phrases (1) • Writing about a building
VOCABULARY DEVELOPMENT A dictionary entry (2) • Countable or uncountable nouns?

READING Famous buildings pp22–23

AIMS

The aim of this section is to help students to think about how they can make notes about a text by extracting the important information. It also introduces students to the language of describing buildings and other structures.

LEAD IN

- Ask:
  – *When do you make notes?*
  Elicit the answer – in lectures, when I'm reading, when I'm revising, etc.
- Ask:
  – *How do you take notes?* and elicit some ideas.
- Focus students' attention on the page and tell students that they are going to read about two famous buildings.

PROCEDURE

1 Students read the instructions. Read through the words in the box with the class and explain any words that students don't understand. Students answer the questions in pairs.

2 Students read the **Study Skill** on making notes. Remind them of the different ways of reading, and point out that we read slowly and carefully when we are making notes.

Students read the instructions. Go through the table quickly. Students then complete the table with the information from the two texts. **O¬ 2**

3 Students label the diagrams with the details from the text. **O¬ 3**

4 Remind students that it is often possible to guess the meaning of new words from their context (**Study Skill** page 17).

Read the instructions with the class and point out that students should first identify the part of speech of the underlined words and then try to guess the meaning. Go through the first question with the class as an example. Students then complete the questions individually. Check answers with the class. **O¬ 4**

5 Read the instructions with the class and remind students that a summary is a short version of a text, containing all the main points. Encourage students to use their notes (and not the text) to complete the summary. **O¬ 5**

6 Read the instructions with the class. Point out that students should use the notes from exercise 2 (and not the text) to write the summary. Tell students to use the summary in exercise 5 as a model. Do the first sentence on the board with the whole class if necessary. Students then complete their summaries individually. **O¬ 6**

READING Answer key pp22–23

O¬ 2

	Taj Mahal	Bank of China Tower
Building		
Built by	Shah Jehan	Ieoh Ming Pei
Located	Agra, north of India	Hong Kong
Date	1631–1654	1982–1990
Building type	a tomb	skyscraper
Made of	white marble, sandstone	glass, steel
Style	Islamic	modern
Notes	Some say–most beautiful building in the world	platform on 42nd floor Can see the whole city

O¬ 3

Taj Mahal: tomb, minarets
Bank of China Tower: 367m, 70 floors

O¬ 4

1 tomb: *noun*
   – a place where the body of an important person is buried
2 symbolizes: *verb*
   – represents something
3 designs: *verb*
   – plans and makes a drawing of something (a building)
4 skyscraper: *noun*
   – a very tall building
5 panoramic: *adjective*
   – of a wide area

O¬ 5

1 Shah Jehan
2 1631
3 1654
4 Agra
5 tomb
6 marble
7 sandstone
8 Islamic

O¬ 6

Students' own answers, but the summary in exercise 5 is a model.

RESEARCH Finding information (2) p23

AIMS

The aim of this section is to give students practice in finding factual information. It encourages them to focus their search and think about the facts that they want to find out. It also prepares students for a later writing task.

LEAD IN

- Discuss the buildings in the article (the Taj Mahal and the Bank of China Tower) with students. Ask:
  – *What do you like, or dislike, about these buildings?*
- Ask them about other buildings that they like – in their country or outside. Get them to give reasons.

PROCEDURE

1 Tell students to read the instructions and look at the list of buildings. They then read the **Study Skill**.

Tell students to choose a building and decide what information they want to find out. Students complete the first column of the table with things they want to find out. They can use the tables about the Taj Mahal and the Bank of China Tower as a guide, but encourage them to use their own ideas (e.g how the building got its name, or what it is used for).

Students then look for information about their building (at home, in the library, or learning centre) and complete the table with notes. Ask them to make a note of their source(s).

Check the notes and the sources in class, and get students to talk about their buildings in pairs. ⊶ 1

EXTENSION ACTIVITY

Get students to think about the two people who built the Taj Mahal and the Bank of China Tower, Shah Jehan and Ieoh Ming Pei. Ask students to choose one of them, or another architect they have heard of.

Ask them to write down five things they would like to find out about this person. Give them a couple of examples of what they could find out: where they were born, where they studied, etc.

Students then search various sources to find answers to their five questions. Check the answers with the class.

WRITING Describing buildings pp24–25

AIMS

The main aim of this section is to prepare students with the vocabulary and structures needed to write paragraphs about buildings. It also aims to develop the skills necessary for more cohesive writing by the use of linking devices, in particular *so* and *because*.

LEAD IN

- Write the words *and* and *but* on the board. Remind students of how they are used to join sentences together (**Study Skill** Linking ideas, page 7).
- Write some example sentences on the board and get students to rewrite them using *and* or *but*. For example:
  – *Lee lives in Berlin. He works in a factory.* (and)
  – *Lee likes going to the cinema. He hates watching TV.* (but)
- Write these pairs of sentences on the board:
  – *Yuki works hard. She needs money.*
  – *Yuki works hard. She is very tired.*
- Elicit that in the first pair, the second sentence shows a reason and in the second pair it shows a result.
- Teach *because* for reason and *so* for result:
  – *Yuki works hard because she needs money.* (reason)
  – *Yuki works hard, so she is very tired.* (result)

PROCEDURE

1 Students read the **Study Skill** on *because*. They then find a sentence with *because* in the text on the Bank of China Tower. **⊙–1**

2 Read the instructions with the class and explain that students should complete the sentences with their own ideas. Elicit possible answers from the class for the first question, e.g. *… it is a very beautiful building, … it is very well known, … they want to take photos.* Students complete the exercise, then compare their answers in pairs. Check answers with the class. **⊙–2**

3 Students read the **Study Skill** on *so*. Point out that we usually put a comma before *so* when it joins sentences.

Students read the instructions and find the sentences with *so* in the texts about the two buildings. **⊙–3**

4 Tell students to read the instructions and the sentences. Deal with any vocabulary difficulties. Students then match the sentences. Check that they have matched the pairs correctly, then tell them to join them using *so*. Check answers with the class. **⊙–4**

5 Students read the instructions and complete the sentences with their own ideas. **⊙–5**

6 Read the instructions with the class and point out that students must choose *because* or *so* to join the sentences.

Students match the sentences and join them using *because* or *so*, then check their answers in pairs. Check answers with the class. **⊙–6**

7 Refer students to the picture and the text. Tell students to read the text quickly, ignoring the gaps.

Students then read the instructions for exercise 7. Read through the words and phrases in the box and explain any that students don't understand. Students then complete the paragraph. Check the answers with the class. **⊙–7**

8 Students read the **Study Skill**. Read through the language in the box with the students and make sure they understand everything.

Students find examples of these words and phrases in the text, and underline them. **⊙–8**

9 Students find a result clause and a reason clause in the text. **⊙–9**

Writing about a building p25

10 Refer students back to the paragraphs about the Taj Mahal and the Bank of China Tower. Tell them to read these and the text about the Tower Houses of Yemen again. They should now look at their notes from page 23 about the building they chose. Ask them to write a description of their building. Remind them to use result and reason clauses. **⊙–10**

EXTENSION ACTIVITY

Ask students to make a table like the one on page 23 (Finding information). Get them to write a list of six things they want to know about Yemen in the left hand column. They should then search for the information and complete the right hand column with notes. Students can then present their results orally to the class or write a few sentences to describe what they found out.

ADDITIONAL PHOTOCOPIABLE ACTIVITY

Writing 4 Describing a place

WRITING Answer key pp24–25

⊙–1
The building is very light inside <u>because</u> it is made of glass and steel.

⊙–2
Possible answers
1 … it is a very beautiful building. 2 … they are afraid of heights.
3 … they are very stressful. 4 … there is not enough rain.
5 … it is very unusual.

⊙–3
It is situated in formal gardens just outside the city, so it is in a very quiet place.
The platform is on the 42nd floor, so visitors can have a panoramic view of the whole city.

⊙–4
1 b Sometimes we just want to get information, so we read the text quickly to find it.
2 e A personal diary is only for ourselves, so we write in a very informal way.
3 a George wants to work for a computer company one day, so he is learning everything about software.
4 d Taxi drivers face traffic jams every day, so they often suffer from stress in their work.
5 c In the summer the oceans are very warm, so this is when hurricanes usually form.

⊙–5
Possible answers
2 … many people come to see it.
3 … it is easy to get to the top.
4 … not many plants grow there.
5 … it is not used for most buildings.
6 … you should visit it in the winter.

⊙–6
1 f I want to visit the Louvre in Paris because it has some beautiful paintings.
2 b Paulo likes climbing mountains, so he is going to Switzerland for his holidays.
3 c Nora wants to work for a newspaper as a journalist because she loves writing and enjoys meeting people.
4 a Land is very expensive in Hong Kong, so most of the buildings are tall and narrow.
5 e India has a lot of rain in the summer months, so it is better to visit the country in the dry season.
6 d In Russia people like to go to their 'dachas' in the summer because they want to get away from the noisy cities and stay in a quiet place.

⊙–7
1 are located 2 so 3 were built 4 are made of 5 have
6 In the centre 7 because 8 there is 9 On the outside
10 There are

⊙–8
<u>there is</u> usually a large sitting room
<u>There are</u> also decorations …
They <u>are made of</u> stone and brick.
They <u>were built</u> by local builders …
The Tower Houses of Yemen <u>are located</u> in the old city …
<u>In the centre of the house</u> is …
There are also decorations <u>around</u> the windows and doors.
On the <u>outside</u> walls …
<u>On the top floor</u> there is usually …

⊙–9
result: …, so many visitors come to Yemen to see them.
reason: … because these floors are for food and animals.

⊙–10
Students' own answers, but the text in exercise 7 is a model.

VOCABULARY DEVELOPMENT
Dictionary work (2) p26

AIMS

This section aims to develop students' dictionary skills. It draws students' attention to the fact that many words in English have more than one meaning and that these are listed in the dictionary. It also encourages the use of a dictionary to check whether nouns are countable (*building*) or uncountable (*oil*).

LEAD IN

- Remind students that dictionaries contain a lot of information, not just the meanings of words. Elicit ideas from the class and write them on the board (e.g. parts of speech, pronunciation, plural forms, examples of use).
- Write the word *cold* on the board. Ask students to give you example sentences and write them down. Try to elicit examples that show the two main meanings of *cold* – a cold temperature (a cold room, a cold day, etc.) and *cold* meaning 'not friendly' (a cold person, a cold look).
- Point out that many words in English have more than one meaning.

PROCEDURE

1 Students read the **Study Skill**. Check that students understand the different meanings of *light*.

Students then find the word *light* in the text on the Bank of China Tower and decide which meaning it is. **⌾ 1**

2 Students now look at the dictionary entries and decide how many meanings there are for each adjective. Check answers, and check that students understand the different meanings. **⌾ 2**

3 Read the instructions and go through the first example with the class.

Students then complete the exercise individually. **⌾ 3**

4 Refer students to the dictionary entries for *rest* and *view*. Make sure they understand the different meanings.

Students find nouns in the texts and check their meanings. **⌾ 4**

5 Remind students that nouns can be countable or uncountable. Read the instructions with the class, then read through the **Study Skill** with the class and check that students understand the difference between countable and uncountable nouns.

Students then look at the words in the box. They check the words in the dictionary and find out if they are countable or uncountable. Check answers with the class. **⌾ 5**

6 Students find the words *glass* and *marble* in their dictionaries and answer the question. **⌾ 6**

VOCABULARY DEVELOPMENT Answer key p26

⌾ 1

The building is very <u>light</u> inside = 1 – full of natural light

⌾ 2

poor: 3 meanings (one is not given here)
rich: 3 meanings
hard: 2 meanings
cool: 3 meanings

⌾ 3

1 a 3, b 1, c 2
2 a 1, b 2
3 a 2, b 3, c 1

⌾ 4

The <u>rest</u> of the building ... = the part that is left
a panoramic <u>view</u> of the whole city = what you can see from a
    place

⌾ 5

information U
floor C
public U
platform C
steel U
rain U
tomb C
garden C

⌾ 6

glass and *marble* can be countable or uncountable according to
    their meaning.

REVIEW p27

AIMS

The aim of this section is to encourage students to review the content of the unit and also to practise and develop the skills they have learnt.

PROCEDURE

1 Tell students to look back at the texts in Unit 4 to find words for building materials. Students complete the diagram in pairs and add their own words.

Draw the diagram on the board and get students to give their answers. **O—⌐ 1**

2 Refer students back to the text on Tower Houses to help them with vocabulary. Students work individually, then check their answers in pairs. **O—⌐ 2**

3 Refer students back to the **Study Skill** on page 25. Students complete the text, using the words and phrases in the box. **O—⌐ 3**

4 Refer students back to the **Study Skills** on page 24. Students join the sentences using either *because* or *so*. Remind them to use a comma before *so*. **O—⌐ 4**

EXTENSION ACTIVITY

Ask students to write a description of a house that they know (their own house, the house of a friend or relative). Get them to draw a plan of the house first.

REVIEW Answer key p27

O—⌐ 1

Possible answers
marble, steel, glass, stone, sandstone, brick + wood, clay, concrete ...

O—⌐ 2

a roof b window c bedroom d second floor e bathroom
f garage g kitchen h stairs i first floor j living room k door
l ground floor m terrace n gate o garden p walls

O—⌐ 3

1 is located
2 was built
3 is made of
4 has
5 On the left
6 on the right
7 There are
8 in the centre
9 around
10 there is

O—⌐ 4

1 Glass is a cheap and light material, so it is used in many modern buildings.
2 Everyone wants to visit the Burj Al Arab because it is a very famous and unusual building.
3 It is important to take good notes because they help you to understand what you read.
4 Shah Jehan decided to build a beautiful tomb for his wife because he loved her so much.
5 Winters in Russia are very cold, so it is important to wear warm clothes.
6 The weather was perfect, so they decided to have lunch in the garden.

5 Education

READING Universities pp28–29

AIMS

This section focuses on prediction. It encourages students to think about the content of a text before they read it, i.e. the topic, the information they can find, and the vocabulary they expect to come across. It also introduces *however* as another way of linking sentences.

LEAD IN

- Ask students about the educational structure of their country, for example, what age children go to school, what types of schools there are, etc.
- Ask at what age students normally go to university in their country.

PROCEDURE

1 Focus students' attention on the pictures and explain that they are all universities. Students read the instructions and answer the questions in pairs. **⌐1**

2 Students read the **Study Skill** and the instructions.

Tell students to read questions 1 to 3 before they skim the title and the first paragraph of the text. Tell students not to read the full text yet. **⌐2**

3 Students read the whole text quickly to check their predictions.

4 Students read the instructions. Remind them to use context to help them to understand the meaning of the words. Students complete the exercise individually, then check their answers in pairs. Check answers with the class. **⌐4**

5 Remind students of the different kinds of reading. Ask them to read the article again slowly and carefully for meaning (intensive or study reading). They should then answer the comprehension questions. Check answers with the class. **⌐5**

6 Students read the **Study Skill** on *however*. Elicit the difference between *but* and *however* (*but* joins two clauses, *however* joins two sentences). Point out the use of commas with *but* and *however*. **⌐6**

Students then read the instructions and answer the questions.

7 Students read the instructions. They then match the sentences and rewrite them using *however*. Remind them to use the correct punctuation. **⌐7**

EXTENSION ACTIVITY

Ask students to write four pairs of sentences using *however*. Let them work with a partner. Two of the examples could be about their present place of study and two about studying or working in another country. Point out that they should compare the good points (advantages) with the bad (disadvantages). Check the examples with the class.

READING Answer key p28–29

⌐1

1 a Moscow State University
  b Harvard University
  c Oxford University
2 and 3 Students' own answers.

⌐2

Possible answers
1 Very young students going to university
2 What is special about the young boy
3 family, intelligent, examinations, school, teachers

⌐4

1 mature
2 genius
3 disagree
4 institution
5 fluent
6 attend

⌐5

1 c 2 b 3 c

⌐6

Possible answers
However, his teachers could see that he was very intelligent.
  (contrast = he couldn't speak English/he was very intelligent)
However, his schoolteachers thought he would have no problems.
  (contrast = he was very young/he would have no problems)
However, are young teenagers really mature enough for university?
  (contrast = young children sometimes go to university/are they mature enough?)

⌐7

1 c Some people think that 14 is too young for university. However, others believe that clever students should not wait.
2 a Yinan Wang was only 14 years old. However, he studied at Oxford University.
3 b At first Yinan Wang could only speak a little English. However, he soon became fluent in the language.

WRITING Formal letters and emails pp 30–31

AIMS

The aim of this section is to make students aware of formal style, especially in formal letters and emails. It prepares students for writing by giving them the conventions and some of the language they will need for simple, routine letters and emails.

LEAD IN

- Ask students to make a list of any emails and letters they have written recently. Ask:
  - *Who did you write these emails and letters to?*
  - *Were they to friends or relatives, or to companies or organizations?*
- Then ask:
  - *How do you write to friends?*
  - *How do you write to people for official reasons?*
  - *Is there any difference?*
- Elicit differences between formal and informal emails and letters, e.g. differences of vocabulary, greetings, etc.
- Introduce the terms *formal* and *informal* language and write these on the board.

PROCEDURE

1 Read the instructions with the class. Students answer the question in pairs. Check answers with the class and write the suggestions on the board. ⊶ 1

2 Students read the **Study Skill**. Point out that these are the conventions in British English. Point out the use of commas after both the greetings and endings. Students then read the instructions and complete the exercise. ⊶ 2

3 Ask students to read the instructions and read the email quickly, ignoring the gaps. Point out that the sender and the date are given automatically, but they should normally write a suitable subject.

Students then complete the exercise. Check answers with the class. ⊶ 3

Students then read the **Study Skills**. Read through the expressions with the class and point out some of the structures which may cause difficulty (e.g. *interested in* + -ing, *look forward to* + -ing) and give examples where needed.

4 Read the instructions and the questions with the class. Explain any vocabulary that students do not understand, e.g. *apply*. Students then read the advertisement and answer the questions. Check answers with the class. ⊶ 4

Writing a letter or email p31

5 Read the instructions with the class. Ask students to look at the email to Mrs Fernandez again and the two **Study Skills** on page 30. Students then complete the writing task. ⊶ 5

EXTENSION ACTIVITY

Ask students to bring in information (a brochure, advertisement, etc.) about a college, university, sports club, cultural society, etc. that interests them. Now ask them to think about what they would like to know about the place and to make notes. They should then write a letter or email to the institution requesting the information they need.

ADDITIONAL PHOTOCOPIABLE ACTIVITY

Writing 5 Drafting and correcting

WRITING Answer key pp30–31

⊶ 1
Possible answers
applying to a university/college
writing to a shop
writing to a teacher/lecturer
writing to a bank or business
writing to a doctor/hospital

⊶ 2
2	Dear Sir/Madam, …	Yours faithfully, …
3	Dear Mrs Thomson, …	Yours sincerely, …
4	Dear Mr Ericson, …	Yours sincerely, …
5	Dear Sir/Madam, …	Yours faithfully, …
6	Dear Dr Darwish, …	Yours sincerely, …
7	Dear Mrs Yamamoto, …	Yours sincerely, …

⊶ 3
1 Dear
2 interested
3 studying
4 please
5 information
6 would
7 know
8 old
9 have
10 diploma
11 hearing
12 sincerely

⊶ 4
Where is the college? In Sydney, Australia
Can you study part-time? Yes
Can you apply online? Yes
Which subject interests you most? Students' own answers.

⊶ 5
Students' own answers, but the email on page 30 is a model.

VOCABULARY DEVELOPMENT Spelling (2) p31

AIMS

This sections aims to focus the students' attention on the spelling rules for forming plurals.

LEAD IN

- Write these nouns on the board: *student, country, watch, mouse.*
- Elicit the plurals of the nouns: *students, countries, watches, mice.*
- Try to elicit rules for plurals from the class.

PROCEDURE

1 Read through the RULES box with the class and make sure students understand everything. Students match the nouns with the rules. **⊙ 1**

2 Read through the words in the box quickly to check that students understand the meanings of the words. Tell students to apply the rules to the words in the box, and use their dictionaries to check. Check answers with the class and point out that *day* just adds *-s* because it has a vowel + *y*, not consonant + *y*. **⊙ 2**

EXTENSION ACTIVITY

Bring in copies of a suitable text, (or choose one of the texts from the book). Get students to look through the text and underline any plural forms. They should then try to classify the plurals according to the rules.

RESEARCH Notes p32

AIMS

The aim of this section is to remind students of the reasons for taking notes. The section also introduces a number of different methods that students can use to take notes while reading.

LEAD IN

- Get students in pairs to think about different ways of taking notes, e.g. a list of points, using diagrams and arrows, etc.
- Elicit ideas from the class, and discuss briefly the advantages (and disadvantages) of different methods.
- Point out that you can use a combination of methods.

PROCEDURE

1 Students try to think of four reasons, then check in the **Study Skill** on page 22. **⊙ 1**

2 Read the **Study Skill** with the class and make sure that students understand everything. Students then match the ways of making notes to the students' notes in exercise 2. **⊙ 2**

3 Students read the text and discuss the question in pairs. **⊙ 3**

4 Students read the text about Harvard University and underline or highlight the important information. Students check their answers in pairs before you check answers with the whole class. **⊙ 4**

5 Ask students to choose an institution (school, college, university) that they want to discuss. They should bring information about the institution to the next class. Students make highlighted notes and then talk about the institutions in pairs. **⊙ 5**

EXTENSION ACTIVITY

Ask students to choose their own text – no more than half a page – on a topic related to their interests. They could choose from a textbook, an article, a web page, etc. They should then underline or highlight the important information and bring the text to the class. Again, ask students to compare their notes with other students and to explain why they have highlighted/underlined certain parts.

VOCABULARY DEVELOPMENT Answer key p31

⊙ 1

1d 2a 3b 4c

⊙ 2

-s: magazines, emails, days
-es: faxes, addresses, viruses, matches
-ies: dictionaries, cities, companies, hobbies
irregular: women, bookshelves, knives

RESEARCH Answer key p32

⊙ 1

understand what you read
remember the important points
write about the topic
revise later for exams

⊙ 2

1c 2d 3b 4a

⊙ 3

Possible answers
The information that is highlighted is the important information. It is mainly facts, e.g. dates, numbers, places.

⊙ 4

Possible answers
private university, founded in 1636, called New College, 1696 named Harvard after John Harvard, became Harvard University 1780, 2,300 professors, 6,700 undergraduate students, 13,600 graduate students, nine faculties

⊙ 5

Students' own answers, but the paragraphs in exercises 3 and 4 are models.

REVIEW p33

AIMS

The aim of this section is to encourage students to review the content of the unit and also to practise and develop the skills they have learnt.

PROCEDURE

1 Tell students to look back at the RULES box on page 31. Students should then apply the rules to the words in the box and complete the table. **⊶ 1**

2 Students should look back at the **Study Skill** on page 29 to help them with this exercise. Remind students to use commas correctly. **⊶ 2**

3 Refer students back to the **Study Skills** on page 30. Students then correct the underlined mistakes and add the missing words. **⊶ 3**

4 Tell students to look back through the unit to find vocabulary related to academic institutions and types of writing. Students complete the diagrams with a partner. **⊶ 4**

5 Students should compare their lists and add further examples. Finally, check answers with the class by filling in the diagrams on the board.

REVIEW   Answer key   pp33

⊶ 1

-s: professors, friends, buildings
-es: geniuses, campuses, classes
-ies: universities, faculties, families
irregular: children, wives, women

⊶ 2

2 f Canada is one of the biggest countries in the world. However, it has a very small population.

3 a Pilots get good salaries. However, they have to spend a lot of time away from home.

4 e Nancy is an excellent cook. However, she usually prefers to eat in the canteen.

5 b The sun is a good source of vitamin D. However, too much can cause skin cancer.

6 c Cars are an important part of modern life. However, they cause a lot of pollution.

⊶ 3

Delgado
to ask
about (on)
is
in
working
interested
you
information
know
hearing
Yours

⊶ 4

Possible answers

academic institutions: university, secondary school, college, institute, academy, primary school, high school

types of writing: letter of application, email, essay, report, note, poem, project, assignment, memo, postcard, exam

6 Technology

READING SKILLS Getting information from websites • Using visuals in a website
WRITING SKILLS Writing definitions • Giving examples • Writing a description of a device
VOCABULARY DEVELOPMENT Homophones
RESEARCH Websites

READING Inventions pp34–35

AIMS

This section aims to develop the students' skimming and scanning skills. It focuses on extracting information from websites, using texts, diagrams, and visuals.

LEAD IN

- Write the word *web* on the board.
- Ask students, in pairs, to use their dictionaries find out:
  a) what part of speech it is
  b) if it has more than one meaning
  c) definitions for each meaning
- Check the answers with the class. Elicit that *web* has two meanings:
  a) The Web = the World Wide Web – *the system that makes it possible for you to see information from all over the world on your computer* – an uncountable noun
  b) web = a spider's web – *a thin net that a spider makes to catch flies* – a countable noun
- Elicit other words related to the Web (*website, web page, webcam*) and ask students to give definitions of these.

PROCEDURE

1 Ask students: *What is an invention?* Listen to students' definitions but do not give an answer at this stage. Elicit examples of inventions. Students then work with a partner and match the inventions with the pictures. Check answers with the class. **⊙━1**

2 Students work with a partner to choose the three most important inventions.

   Ask each pair to give their three most important inventions and explain why they chose them. Draw a table on the board with the inventions (a–j) in the first column. Draw three more columns and give them the headings 1st, 2nd, 3rd. Add the answers of each pair to the table (by ticking the appropriate square) and get the results for the class as a whole. Discuss the results briefly.

   Elicit other examples of important inventions that are not on the list. **⊙━2**

3 Students read the definition of *invention*. Compare it to the definitions of *invention* they gave earlier. Students then write a definition of *device*. Check answers with the class. Write the best definitions on the board. Tell students to find a definition in a dictionary, and compare this to the class definitions. **⊙━3**

4 Students read the **Study Skill**. Remind students of the meaning of the terms *skimming* and *scanning*. Students scan the website article to answer the question. **⊙━4**

5 Tell students to read the instructions and the headings. Students should now skim the article to match the headings with the paragraphs. Students check their answers in pairs before you check answers with the whole class. **⊙━5**

6 Students read the **Study Skill**. Point out that visuals are an important part of a text. They can help you to understand the text fully. Students then read the instructions and complete the exercise. Draw the diagram on the board and get students to label it. Ask one or two students to give a short explanation of how the system works, referring to the diagram on the board. **⊙━6**

7 Students read the instructions. Remind students to use the context of the words to help understand the meaning. Students complete the exercise. **⊙━7**

READING Answer key pp34–35

⊙━1
a the aeroplane
b satellites
c radio
d the computer
e the car
f television
g the washing machine
h the Internet
i the telephone
j the printing press

⊙━2
Students' own answers.

⊙━3

Possible answers
A device is a tool or piece of equipment that you use for doing a special job, for example a tin-opener or a remote control.

⊙━4
Sat Nav = Satellite Navigation

⊙━5
a Paragraph 3
b Paragraph 4
c Paragraph 1
d Paragraph 2

⊙━6
a satellite
b radio signal
c ground station
d receiver

⊙━7
1 launched
2 calculates
3 portable
4 destination
5 accurate
6 orbiting
7 locate

WRITING Describing things pp36–37

AIMS
The main aim of this section is to enable students to write descriptions of devices, to explain how they work, and to say what their uses are. The section also teaches students to write simple definitions and example sentences.

LEAD IN
- Choose a device that you or one of the students have in your bag, e.g. a calculator, mobile phone, or watch. Elicit a description of the device from the class, i.e. information about its size, its weight, the cost, its uses, and how it works.
- Ask the class to try to write a definition, working in pairs.
- Listen to some of the definitions and write them on the board.

PROCEDURE
1 Students read the **Study Skill** on definitions. They then read the instructions and complete the exercise. **⊙ₙ1**

2 Read the exercise with the class and do the first sentence as an example. Point out that *which* and *that* are interchangeable in these sentences. **⊙ₙ2**

3 Students complete the definitions, using their own words. Tell students to check their answers with the dictionary entries. **⊙ₙ3**

EXTENSION ACTIVITY
Let students choose three or four other devices that they are familiar with. They should then write definitions of them as in the examples. Get students to check their definitions in a dictionary.

4 Students read the **Study Skill** on giving examples. Point out the use of commas in the sentences with *for example* and *such as*. Also refer them to the use of *e.g.* as an abbreviation of *for example*.

Students now read the instructions and complete the exercise. **⊙ₙ4**

5 Students read the instructions and the sentences. Do the first sentence on the board, eliciting examples of makes of television from the class. Students then complete the exercise. **⊙ₙ5**

6 Read the instructions with the class and make sure that students understand the word *laptop*. Point out the picture of the woman with the laptop. Students read the instructions and complete the paragraph. Check the answers with the class. **⊙ₙ6**

Writing a description of a device p37

7 Read the instructions with the class and read through the list of devices in the box. Explain any vocabulary that students don't understand. Students then choose a device and make notes on it. Encourage them to use various sources to collect their information. Ask them to make a note of their source(s), i.e. the website, the book, the newspaper article, etc.

Check their notes and then ask a few students to give a brief talk about their devices using their notes. **⊙ₙ7**

8 Read through the paragraph about laptop computers again with the class. Point out the definition (*Laptops are a type of …*) and the way examples are given. Elicit the fact that it contains a description of the size and weight of a laptop and an explanation of how it works. It also explains why they are popular and where they can be used. Students then read the instructions and write their own paragraph about the device they chose in exercise 7, using their notes. **⊙ₙ8**

9 Students read the instructions and correct the mistakes in the paragraph. Check the answers with the class. Make sure students understand why the underlined words are wrong. Explain the grammar/spelling rules as necessary. **⊙ₙ9**

10 Students read the instructions, then go back and check their own work.

WRITING Answer key pp36–37

⊙ₙ1
1 A thermometer is an instrument **which** measures temperature.
2 A satellite is an object **that** circles another object.
3 A vacuum cleaner is a machine **which** cleans carpets.
4 A laptop is a type of computer **that** is portable and weighs about 1–3kg.

⊙ₙ2
1 c A photocopier is a machine which/that makes copies of documents, such as letters.
2 b A remote control is a device which/that controls things, such as televisions, from a distance.
3 d A drill is a tool which/that you use for making holes.
4 e A speedometer is an instrument which/that tells you how fast you are travelling in a car or plane.
5 a An iPod is a type of MP3 player which/that is made by Apple.

⊙ₙ3
Possible answers
1 A calculator is an instrument that/which you use for calculating numbers.
2 A fax machine is a machine that/which uses telephone lines to send copies of letters, etc.
3 A microwave is a type of oven that/which cooks or heats food very quickly.
4 A laser is a machine that/which makes a very strong line of light.

⊙ₙ4
Paragraph 1   Modern Sat Nav devices, for example the popular Garmin …
For example, they can even tell you the names …
Paragraph 4   They think we might be in danger of losing some important skills, such as reading maps.

⊙ₙ5
Possible answers
1 … Sony, Panasonic, Toshiba, etc.
2 … can use it to locate our position.
3 … mobile phones or satellite television
4 … such as a Ferrari, a Lotus

⊙ₙ6
1 type
2 which
3 example
4 so
5 but
6 because
7 such as

⊙ₙ7
Students' own answers.

⊙ₙ8
Students' own answers, but the text in exercise 6 is a model.

⊙ₙ9
A satellite is any object <u>which</u> orbits another object. All bodies that <u>are</u> part of the solar system, for <u>example</u> the Earth and Jupiter, <u>are satellites</u>. Most <u>of</u> these bodies orbit the sun, but others orbit planets. For example, the moon <u>orbits</u> the Earth. When we <u>use</u> the term 'satellite', we <u>usually</u> mean an artificial satellite. This <u>is</u> a man-made <u>object</u> that orbits the Earth, or <u>another</u> body. However, <u>scientists</u> may also use the term for natural satellites, or moons.

VOCABULARY DEVELOPMENT Spelling (3) p37

AIMS
This section aims to make students aware of homophones, by looking at pairs of homophones which regularly cause confusion.

LEAD IN
- Write the words *right* and *write* on the board.
- Elicit that they have the same sound, but the spelling and meaning are different.
- Explain that these words are homophones, i.e. they sound the same, but have different spellings and different meanings.
- Ask them for other examples of homophones. Give one or two examples, if students cannot think of any: e.g.*wait/weight, sea/see.*

PROCEDURE
1 Students read the **Study Skill**. Read through the examples at the bottom of the box and check that students understand the difference between the homophones. Students then complete the gap-fill exercise. **O─ 1**

RESEARCH Websites p38

AIMS
This section aims to encourage students to be more critical of websites. It helps them to recognise the different types of website and to check their authorship, accuracy, and reliability.

LEAD IN
- Ask students:
  – *What is a website?* – *Who creates websites?*   – *Why do people have websites?*
- Elicit discussion and bring out the point that there are many different types of website written by various people. For example, some belong to organizations, some are the work of individuals, and some are used to advertise products.
- Make the point that not all websites are useful or reliable.

PROCEDURE
1 Students read the **Study Skill** on reliable sources. Go through the points in the box with the students and discuss any difficulties.

Tell students to read the instructions and the questions below. Give students time to look over the three examples of websites and answer the questions. Get them to check their answers with a partner. **O─ 1**

BACKGROUND INFORMATION – WIKIPEDIA
Wikipedia describes itself as:

a free, web-based, collaborative, multilingual encyclopedia project supported by the non-profit Wikimedia Foundation. The Wikimedia Foundation operates some of the largest collaboratively-edited reference projects in the world, including Wikipedia, one of the 20 most visited websites.

Since its creation in 2001, Wikipedia has rapidly grown into the largest reference website on the Internet. The content of Wikipedia is free, written collaboratively by people from all around the world. This website is a wiki, which means that *anyone* with access to an Internet-connected computer can edit, correct, or improve information throughout the encyclopedia, simply by clicking the *edit this page* link (with a few minor exceptions, such as protected articles and the main page).

Point out that Wikipedia is a very convenient tool for finding information. However, because anyone can edit information in the encyclopaedia, it is best to check any information in Wikipedia with other sources.

2 Students read the instructions and the list of topics in the box. Students choose their topic from the list and try to find three different websites related to the topic. Explain that they should try to find websites which are quite different from one another. Give them time to do the research and report back to the class.

Students could do the research in pairs or small groups, with one student reporting back to the class on behalf of the pair or group. **O─ 2**

VOCABULARY DEVELOPMENT Answer key p37

O─ 1
1 know, no
2 It's
3 too, to
4 There, their, They're

RESEARCH Answer key p38

O─ 1
1 a online encyclopaedia (Wikipedia)
   b company website (North Energy)
   c someone's personal page
2 The best website is the online encyclopaedia (the company website may not be objective, the personal page contains opinions and may not be reliable)

O─ 2
Students' own answers.

Writing 6 Internet research task

REVIEW p39

AIMS

The aim of this section is to encourage students to review the content of the unit and also to practise and develop the skills they have learnt.

PROCEDURE

1 Refer students back to the **Study Skill** on writing definitions on page 36. They then read the instructions and complete the reordering exercise. The first could be done with the class as an example. 🔑 1

2 Students read the instructions and the list of words in the box. Tell students to use their dictionaries to check the meaning of words they do not know. Encourage students to add some extra words to each list.

Draw the table on the board and use it to check the answers with the whole class. 🔑 2

3 Refer students back to the exercises in Unit 6 to help them with vocabulary. Students complete the text using words and phrases from the box. 🔑 3

REVIEW Answer key p39

🔑 1

1 Gold is a metal which is used to make jewellery.
2 A washing machine is a machine that washes clothes.
3 An elephant is a very large animal which lives in Africa.
4 A hurricane is a tropical storm that causes a lot of damage.
5 A robot is a kind of machine that works like a person.

🔑 2

transport: the metro, an aeroplane, a train + a car, a bike ...
work/study: a fax machine, a photocopier, a printer + a computer, a desk ...
home: a washing machine, a dishwasher, a microwave + a television, a vacuum cleaner ...

🔑 2

1 portable
2 lost
3 accurate
4 calculate
5 launch
6 exactly
7 network
8 distance
9 device
10 locate

READING SKILLS Topic sentences • Writer's opinion
WRITING SKILLS Punctuation (2) • Linking ideas (6) • Using pronouns • Writing about food and drink
VOCABULARY DEVELOPMENT Prefixes

READING Food from other countries pp40–41

AIMS

This unit focuses on topic sentences and the role they play in the organization of a paragraph. Its helps students to identify topic sentences and to use them to get the meaning from texts quickly. It also aims to make students think about the writer and the need to identify his or her personal views while reading a text.

LEAD IN

- Ask students to describe the national dish of their country and say what it is made of. Teach the word *ingredients*.
- Ask:
  – *Where do the ingredients come from?* – *Are they all from the local area?*
  – *Are they from other countries?*
- Make the point that some ingredients come from other countries.

PROCEDURE

1 Read the instructions with the class and make sure that students understand the word *local*. Read through the items of food to check understanding. Students work in small groups and complete the table. **⊙┐1**

2 Remind students of the need to predict what will be in a text – the topic, the information they will find, and some likely vocabulary.

  Students read the title of the text and look at the map, then try to answer the questions. Check the students' suggestions, but do not give answers at this stage. **⊙┐2**

3 Remind students of what *scanning* means. Students scan the text and underline the definition. **⊙┐3**

4 Students read the **Study Skill** on topic sentences. Refer students to the text and point out that the topic sentences are missing. Read through the instructions and the topic sentences with the class. Check that students understand everything.

  Remind students that they should only skim the article, not read it carefully. Students match the topic sentences to the paragraphs individually, then check their answers in pairs. **⊙┐4**

5 Read the instructions and the example with the class and remind students what *context* means. Students complete the exercise. Check answers with the class. **⊙┐5**

6 Read the instructions and the three sentences with the class. Students read the **Study Skill**. Point out that it is important to distinguish between fact and opinion in a text. Point out that sometimes a writer's opinion is clearly marked (*I think, I believe, It seems to me,* etc.). However, other times what is opinion and what is fact is not so clear.

  Students decide which sentence shows the writer's opinion. **⊙┐6**

EXTENSION ACTIVITY

Ask students to look back at some of the texts in earlier units, for example *Too young for Oxford?* in Unit 5 or *Lost? No – I've got my Sat Nav!* in Unit 6. Tell students to read the texts again and see if they can find sentences showing the writer's opinion. Discuss their answers as a class.

7 Remind students that a summary is a short version of a text which contains the main ideas.

  Read through the words in the box with the class and explain any words students don't understand. Students then complete the summary. Check answers with the class. **⊙┐7**

READING Answer key pp40–41

⊙┐1

Students' own answers.

⊙┐2

Possible answers
1 how many miles food travels
2 information about where food comes from
3 farmer, market, fresh, aeroplanes, distance

⊙┐3

A food mile is the distance that food travels from the farmer's field to the person who buys the food.

⊙┐4

a 4   b 2   c 1   d not needed   e 3

⊙┐5

Possible answers
1 consumer: the person who buys the food
2 disadvantages: some bad things about the system
3 available: we can get them
4 imported: coming from other countries

⊙┐6

Sentence 2 shows the writer's opinion.

⊙┐7

1 distance
2 consumer
3 local
4 disadvantage
5 season
6 Nowadays
7 imported
8 because
9 petrol
10 pollution

EXTENSION ACTIVITY

Get students to read paragraph 3 again and to look at the map. Tell them to work in pairs and prepare a description of what the map shows. Get some students to describe the trade routes on the map to the class.

Now ask the class to prepare a similar map to show imports to their own country. Choose some of the food items from the list, or other well-known food items. Give students the task of finding out the countries of origin of these products. Place a world map on the classroom wall. When students have finished their research, they add arrows and notes to the map.

WRITING Describing food and drink pp42–43

AIMS

The main aim of this section is to help students to write paragraphs describing food and drink, and to use topic sentences in their own writing. This section also shows students other ways in which ideas can be linked in writing – by the use of pronouns and the linking phrase *in addition*.

LEAD IN

- Remind students of some of the uses of commas shown so far in the book, e.g. before *so* and *but* and after *However*.
- Write some examples on the board:
  – *She lives in Hong Kong, but she was born in Beijing.*
  – *The GPS is portable, so you can put it in your pocket.*
  – *Mike studies French. However, he only understands a little.*
- Now write on the board a sentence containing a list of items, but with punctuation missing, for example:
  – *I am studying English information technology business studies and mathematics*
- Ask students to write out the sentence with punctuation.
- See what answers they have given, without giving the correct answer, before moving on to the first exercise.

BACKGROUND INFORMATION – COMMAS

We use commas as an aid to understanding. In longer sentences they may indicate where a reader can take a breath. The following are a few of the more important uses of commas:

a) Before certain conjunctions – but, so, or … (but not usually in front of and). For example,
   – *I am from Argentina, but I am living in London at the moment.*
b) After sequencing words – first, after that, finally, …
   – *Finally, she checks the essay for any spelling or grammar mistakes.*
c) After other linking words
   – *However, the experiment was not successful.*
d) In formal letters and emails
   – *Dear Dr Patel, … Yours sincerely,*
e) Separating items in a list: *My brother likes swimming, fishing, and reading.* (The use of a comma before *and* is possible – it is a stylistic variation.)
   Point out to students that a full stop, and not a comma, is used to end a sentence.

PROCEDURE

1 Students read the **Study Skill** and punctuate the sentences. Check answers with the class. Explain that a comma before *and* is optional. **⚷ 1**

Point out that a colon can be used to introduce a list, for example in sentence 3.

EXTENSION ACTIVITY

Ask students to write four true sentences that include lists. Give them the beginning of the sentences.
– *My favourite … are …*
– *My (sister/brother/friend …) speaks … languages:*
– *The ingredients of … are …*
– *… is studying (physics, …)*

WRITING Answer key pp42–43

⚷ 1

1 Danny's favourite foods are pizza, chocolate, burgers, and ice-cream.
2 The three materials used in the building were glass, concrete, and steel.
3 Parwin speaks five languages fluently: Farsi, English, Urdu, Turkish, and French.
4 For the experiment you will need water, salt, a bowl, and a small piece of paper.
5 The ingredients of a Spanish omelette are onions, eggs, potatoes, and salt.

2 Read the **Study Skill** with the class. Make sure students understand the difference between *in addition* and *and*.

Students find two examples of *in addition* in the article on page 41. 🔑 **2a**

Students now match the sentences and rewrite them using *in addition*. Remind them to use commas correctly. 🔑 **2b**

3 Read the instructions with the class and remind students what a topic sentence is. Check answers and ask the students to write out the sentences to form a paragraph. 🔑 **3**

4 Students read the **Study Skill**. Check that they understand everything. Elicit some other examples of pronouns from the class, e.g. personal pronouns and possessive pronouns. Students now read the instructions and replace the nouns in the sentences with the pronouns in the box. 🔑 **4**

5 Read the instructions with the class. Elicit that mint tea is an example of a drink identified with a culture. Students complete the paragraph with the missing pronouns. 🔑 **5**

Writing about food and drink p43

6 Tell students to read the instructions. Point out that they are writing for a foreign visitor, who probably knows very little about their culture. Get them to think about the ingredients, how it is made, when it is eaten or drunk, etc. They should discuss their ideas with a partner and make notes.

Students then write a paragraph. Check the paragraphs. They could be displayed as part of a project on local culture. 🔑 **6**

ADDITIONAL PHOTOCOPIABLE ACTIVITY

Writing 7 Topic sentences and identifying main ideas

🔑 **2a**

Paragraph 2: In addition, they could only get food ...
Paragraph 4: In addition, food that travels a long way ...

🔑 **2b**

1 c   Aeroplanes cause a lot of air pollution. In addition, they make a lot of noise when they land and take off.
2 d   Food that travels a long distance is not very fresh. In addition, it is very expensive because of the costs of transport.
3 b   Shopping in local markets is more interesting. In addition, the food is usually cheaper than in supermarkets.
4 a   The climate is very hot in Saudi Arabia. In addition, there is very little rainfall.

🔑 **3**

a 2   b 5   c 3   d 6   e 1 (topic sentence)   f 4

🔑 **4**

1 it
2 them
3 They
4 His
5 Her, she

🔑 **5**

Topic sentence: The most important drink in Morocco is mint tea.

1 It
2 they
3 it
4 them
5 them
6 It

🔑 **6**

Students' own answers, but the paragraph in exercise 5 is a model.

VOCABULARY DEVELOPMENT
Prefixes and their meanings p44

AIMS
The aim of this section is to focus students' attention on the use of prefixes, in particular, negative prefixes.

LEAD IN
- Write the word *happy* on the board. Ask the class for the meaning of the word.
- Now write *unhappy* and again ask for the meaning.
- Point out that *un-* is a prefix – a negative prefix.
- Try to elicit other examples of negative prefixes.

PROCEDURE
1 Students read the **Study Skill** and complete the definition of a prefix using their dictionaries. **⚷ 1**

2 Read through the sentences briefly and draw students' attention to the different prefixes. Students then match the underlined words with the meanings. Students check their answers in pairs. **⚷ 2**

3 Students should look at the negative prefixes in the box. Then ask them to complete the sentences with the appropriate prefix. Check answers with the class. **⚷ 3**

4 Students match the underlined words with their meanings. **⚷ 4**

REVIEW p45

AIMS
The aim of this section is to encourage students to review the content of the unit and also to practise and develop the skills they have learnt.

PROCEDURE
1 Write the word *teacher* on the board and underline the vowels *ea*. Point out to students that words with two vowels are common in English. They can cause spelling problems.

   Students read the instructions and complete the exercise. Check answers with the class. **⚷ 1**

2 Refer students to the title of the article and the pictures. Ask students what they know about coffee (e.g. where it grows, how we make a cup of coffee).

   Refer students back to the **Study Skill** on topic sentences (page 40). Students then read the instructions and match the topic sentences with the paragraphs. There is one extra sentence. Check the answers with the class. **⚷ 2**

3 Refer students back to the **Study Skill** on page 44.

   Put students in pairs to complete this exercise. Point out that they can use words from the unit or other words they know.

   To check the answers, draw the diagrams on the board and add the students' answers. **⚷ 3**

4 Students use their dictionaries to add other words to the lists. Check the answers with the class. **⚷ 4**

VOCABULARY DEVELOPMENT Answer key p44

⚷ 1

Possible answer
A prefix is a group of letters that you add to the beginning of a word to change its meaning.

⚷ 2

1d 2f 3c 4e 5a 6b

⚷ 3

1 unhappy
2 disliked
3 irregular
4 impossible
5 incomplete
6 immoral
7 inaccurate
8 disorganized, untidy

⚷ 4

1e 2d 3c 4a 5b

REVIEW Answer key p45

⚷ 1

1 ingredients
2 onions
3 measure
4 season
5 around
6 contains
7 countries
8 bread
9 field
10 building
11 reason
12 materials

⚷ 2

a3 b not needed c2 d1

⚷ 3

Possible answers
im-: impossible, impatient, impolite, immoral, immobile, immature
in-: incorrect, inaccurate, incomplete, informal, independent, inexperienced
dis-: distrust, disagree, disagreement, disorganised, disadvantage, dishonest
un-: unhelpful, unhappy, untidy, unusual, unfriendly, unsuccessful

⚷ 4

Students' own answers.

8 Cities of the world

READING SKILLS Looking at data • Getting facts from a text
WRITING SKILLS Comparatives and superlatives • Linking ideas (7) • Writing about cities
RESEARCH Finding facts and figures
VOCABULARY DEVELOPMENT Word-attack skills

READING City life pp46–47

AIMS

This section focuses on data in a text. It looks at various ways data can be shown visually, for example in tables, charts, and graphs. It shows students how to interpret the data in visuals, and how visuals can improve their understanding of a text.

LEAD IN

- Write the word *data* on the board and ask students what it means. Elicit the words *facts, information, numbers, statistics.*
- Write on the board: *The data is/are very interesting.* Point out that the word *data* can be considered as a plural noun or an uncountable noun.
- Then ask students:
  – *How can we show data visually?*
- Try to elicit the terms *table, graph, flow chart*, etc.

PROCEDURE

1 Put students into pairs or small groups and ask them to look at the words in the list. Check that they understand the meanings. Read the instructions with the class and give students time to work out the order.

Collect the results for the class and put them into a table on the board. Briefly discuss the issues with the class. **On 1**

2 Students now stay in their pairs or groups and discuss which city they would most like to live in. Ask them to take into account the factors in the previous exercise. Get the class together to see what cities they decided on. Find out what reasons they give for their choice. **On 2**

BACKGROUND INFORMATION – READING

The information used in the ranking in the reading text was based on a report from the Economist Intelligence Unit, which produces a ranking of world cities based on the following categories: healthcare, stability, culture and environment, education, and infrastructure. A summary is available on Wikipedia, World's most livable cities, http://en.wikipedia.org/wiki/World's_most_livable_cities

3 Tell students to read the **Study Skill**. Get them to identify each type of visual. Draw their attention briefly to the tables in the texts on pages 46 and 47.

Students should now read the instructions and the four questions. Students scan the article and find the information. Check answers with the class. **On 3**

4 Students should look through the text again to find the names of the missing cities and complete the table. **On 4**

5 Read the instructions and then go through the questions briefly with the students. Tell them to read the text slowly and carefully to find the answers to the questions. Check answers and discuss the answer to question 3 as a class. **On 5**

6 Students read the **Study Skill**. Read the instructions with the class and point out that students should look at the visuals as well as the text to find the answers. Check answers with the class. **On 6**

READING Answer key pp46–47

On 1

Students' own answers.

On 2

Students' own answers.

On 3

1 The Economist Intelligence Unit
2 140 cities
3 Vancover
4 Osaka, Tokyo, Singapore, and Hong Kong

On 4

1 Vancover
2 Vienna
3 Melbourne
4 Toronto
5 Calgary
6 Helsinki
7 Sydney
8 Perth
9 Adelaide
10 Auckland

On 5

Possible answers
1 They came in the middle of the list.
   Reasons: Transport and crime are problems with these cities.
2 They have good transport, low crime rates, and a good climate.
3 Students' own answers.

On 6

1 Pacific Ocean
2 22° C
3 Yes, on the mountains
4 November
5 580,000 (Vancouver City), 2 million in the region
6 Chinese
7 After a British naval captain, George Vancouver
8 The Lookout, Harbour Centre Tower

WRITING Comparing data pp48–49

AIMS

This section aims to help students analyse data. It focuses on the comparison of data and reviews the comparative and superlative form of adjectives.

It also shows how writing can be improved by using the relative pronouns *which* and *where* to form non-defining relative clauses. It prepares students to write about cities.

LEAD IN

- Bring a world map (or a globe) into the class.
- Write the names of the cities Toronto and Moscow on the board. Ask students to locate the cities on the map.
- Point out that the two cities have similar latitudes and both are located inland.
- Ask students what they think the climate is like in these two cities.

PROCEDURE

1 Ask students in pairs to study the data in the charts. Check that they can differentiate between the data for Moscow and that for Toronto. Make sure they can read the scales on the vertical axes (rainfall in mm and temperature in °C).

Students should now read the sentences and decide if they are true or false. Ask them to correct the false sentences. Go over the first two sentences with the students as examples. Then give them time to complete the exercise and check the answers. **⊙━1**

2 Students read the instructions and underline the comparative and superlative forms. Do the first sentence as an example. **⊙━2**

3 Read the RULES box with the class and make sure students understand everything. Read the instructions with the class and tell students to copy the table to their notebooks. They then complete the table with the correct forms of the adjectives.

Draw a table on the board and use it to check the answers and the spelling with the class. **⊙━3**

EXTENSION ACTIVITY

Ask the students to research data about a city they know, for example the city they live in or the nearest city. They should find out:

- the hottest month
- the coldest month
- the wettest month
- the driest month

Ask them to write six sentences about their data using comparative and superlative forms.

4 Read the instructions with the class and go through the tables to make sure that students understand everything. Students then complete the paragraph using the statistics in the table and the adjectives in the box. **⊙━4**

5 Read the **Study Skill** with the class and make sure that students understand everything.

Students now read the instructions and complete the exercise. **⊙━5**

ADDITIONAL PHOTOCOPIABLE ACTIVITY

Writing 8 Describing similarities and differences

Writing about cities p49

6 Refer students to the notes and ask what they know about Mumbai.

Students now read the notes and use them to complete the paragraph. Check answers with the class. **⊙━6**

7 Read the instructions with the class and do the first question as an example if necessary. Students rewrite the paragraph. **⊙━7**

WRITING Answer key pp48–49

⊙━1

1 T   2 T   3 F (July is the wettest month)   4 T
5 F (Toronto is hotter)   6 T   7 F (July is the hottest month)   8 T

⊙━2

1 wetter   2 drier   3 wettest   4 driest   5 hotter   6 colder
7 hottest   8 coldest

⊙━3

dry – drier – the driest
cold – colder – the coldest
hot – hotter – the hottest
friendly – more friendly – the most friendly (friendlier/friendliest is also possible)
popular – more popular – the most popular
mild – milder – the mildest
difficult – more difficult – the most difficult
cool – cooler – the coolest
big – bigger – the biggest
nice – nicer – the nicest
low – lower – the lowest

⊙━4

1 biggest
2 127 (or 130)
3 49 (or 50)
4 smallest
5 highest
6 14
7 lowest
8 7.64
9 higher
10 lower.

⊙━5

1 Melbourne, which is one of the largest cities in Australia, came second in the survey.
2 The highest-ranking cities in Asia were Osaka and Tokyo, which is the capital of Japan.
3 Chinatown, where there are many good restaurants, is located near the centre of the city.
4 On Monday we visited the Grand Bazaar in Istanbul, where you can buy everything from carpets to gold chains.

⊙━6

1 Bombay
2 west
3 hot
4 monsoon
5 18m
6 film
7 1668
8 British East India
9 Museum

⊙━7

Mumbai, which is also known as Bombay, lies on the west coast of India. The best time to visit is during the months of December, January, and February, **which are usually cool and dry**. The spring is very hot and the summers are wet because this is the monsoon season. The city has a population of 20 million people, **which makes it the largest city in India**. It is famous for its very successful film industry, **which is called Bollywood**, and its port. It is also an important commercial centre. The city was founded in 1668 by the British East India Company. There are many sights to see in Mumbai, including the Mani Bhavan Museum and the famous Chowpatty beach, **where the people of Mumbai like to walk in the evenings**.

RESEARCH Researching a city p50

AIMS

This section helps students use the Internet to get specific information. It encourages them to make notes of sources and provides them with some useful websites to help with their searches for information.

LEAD IN

- Write the name *Rio de Janeiro* on the board. Ask:
  – *How can you get facts and figures about Rio de Janeiro, such as population, climate, economy, etc?*
- Discuss students' ideas.

PROCEDURE

1 Students read the **Study Skill**. They should then read the instructions and think about a city they would like to research. Ask students to choose different cities. Refer students to the table and check that they understand all the vocabulary in it.

Give students time outside the class to search for information on their chosen cities. Remind them to find information that is accurate and up-to-date.

Choose a few students to report to the class on the information they have found. Check that they have made a note of the website, books, etc. that they have used.

2 Ask students to read again about Mumbai. They should now use their notes from exercise 1 to write a paragraph about the city they chose.

The corrected paragraphs could be used, together with photos of the cities and a world map, as a class display. 🔑 2

VOCABULARY DEVELOPMENT New words p50

AIMS

This section aims to teach students how to deal with new words by analysing the structure, i.e. using word-attack skills. It points out how they can often understand an unfamiliar word by breaking it down into its component parts.

LEAD IN

- Ask students to brainstorm ways of understanding new words that they meet, e.g. using a dictionary, guessing the meaning from context, finding an explanation in the text.
- Explain to students that they are now going to learn a new skill.

PROCEDURE

1 Read through the **Study Skill** with the class and make sure that students understand everything. Elicit from the class that *renamed* means 'given a new or different name'.

Read the instructions with the task and make sure students understand what they have to do. Students complete the exercise. 🔑 1

EXTENSION ACTIVITY

Select a text of a suitable level and content. Ask students to look through the text and underline three unfamiliar words (or select words for them). They should then try to use word-attack skills on the words.

RESEARCH Answer key p50

🔑 2

Students' own answers, but the paragraph on Mumbai is a model.

VOCABULARY DEVELOPMENT Answer key p50

🔑 1

1 un-count-able = adjective, for nouns that we cannot count
2 re-take = verb, to take again
3 dis-organize-d = adjective, not organized
4 re-built = verb, built again
5 un-recognize-able = adjective, for things that we can't recognize

REVIEW p51

AIMS

The aim of this section is to encourage students to review the content of the unit and also to practise and develop the skills they have learnt.

PROCEDURE

1 Students read the instructions. Refer students back to the **Study Skill** on page 46 to help them. Students complete the exercise. Draw the diagram on the board and check the answers with the class. ⊶ 1

2 Refer students back to the **Study Skill** on page 49. Students then read the instructions and complete the exercise. Do the first sentence with the class as an example if necessary. ⊶ 2

3 Students read the instructions and complete the exercise, using their own ideas. ⊶ 3

4 Refer students back to the RULES box on comparative and superlative forms (page 48).

Students read the instructions and the example sentence, and look at the table. They then write five sentences about the data in the table. Check answers and write some of the students' example sentences on the board. ⊶ 4

5 Divide the class into small groups (teams) and use the quiz in class as a general knowledge quiz. Give each team time to complete the quiz and then check the answers.

Alternatively, if sources are available, for example in a learning centre or computer lab, get the students to find out the answers from suitable books, encyclopaedias, or websites. ⊶ 5

REVIEW Answer key p51

⊶ 1

Possible answers

visuals: table, pie chart, bar chart, graph, flow chart, diagram, picture, drawing

⊶ 2

1 e New York, which is located on Manhattan Island, is the best-known city in North America.
2 d Port Moresby, which is the capital of Papua New Guinea, has a very high crime rate.
3 c In Vancouver you can go skiing in the mountains, which surround the city and are covered in snow in the winter.
4 b Robson Street, which is the main shopping street for fashion, is well worth a visit.
5 a London is famous for its beautiful parks, which are located near the centre of the city.

⊶ 3

Possible answers

1 ..., where they like to go for walks.
2 ..., where people meet to have tea and coffee.
3 ..., where the national football team plays, ...
4 ..., where people like to go for dinner.
5 ..., where you can go on boat trips.

⊶ 4

Possible answers

1 Russia has a higher birth rate than Germany.
2 Turkey has the highest birth rate.
3 Germany has a smaller population than Russia.
4 Germany has a bigger population than Turkey.
5 Turkey has the smallest population.

⊶ 5

1   Tokyo *
2   32,450,000 *
3 a Rio de Janeiro (1101.1 mm in a year) is wetter than Lisbon (702.4mm).
4 d Berlin
5 a Madrid   b Lahore   c San Francisco
6 a Damascus
7 b Nairobi
8 d Bangkok

Note: Different sources give different population statistics depending on whether they are taking the official city boundary, or the built up area. The figure here is for the largest urban area.

9 Brain power

READING SKILLS In other words • Making notes (3)
WRITING SKILLS Common mistakes • Summaries • Writing a summary
RESEARCH Books

READING A healthy brain pp52–53

AIMS

The aim of this unit is to give students further practice in getting information from a text by taking notes. Students are helped to complete linear notes (using a list of points).

Students are also made aware of how writers use synonyms or rephrasing to avoid repeating words. This improves the style of the writing. Students are taught to look out for rephrasing when they read as it can help them to understand any new words and expressions.

LEAD IN

- Ask students to clench both fists and to hold them together so that the fingers are facing each other. Demonstrate to the class.
- Now ask them to turn to their neighbour and to hold their fists at head height. Point out that their fists represent the approximate size of the human brain.
- Now ask:
  – *What do you know about the brain?*   – *What it is made of? What protects it?*
- Write the students' ideas on the board, but do not give any answers at this point.

PROCEDURE

1 Tell students to read the instructions and look through the questions in the quiz. Deal with any difficulty with the questions. Then give students time to try to answer the questions individually. When most students have answers to the questions, stop the exercise. Do not go over the answers at this point.

2 Students read the *Brain facts* to check their answers. **⟳ 2**

3 Read the instructions with the class and make sure students are clear what a topic sentence is.

Students should now skim the article and match the topic sentences to the paragraphs. **⟳ 3**

4 Students read the **Study Skill**. Point out to students that they can look for rephrasing in texts to help them understand new words. Students find the rephrasing of *healthy* (in good shape) and *delicate* (easily damaged).

Students now complete the exercise. **⟳ 4**

5 Ask students what they have already learned about making notes. Refer them back to the **Study Skills** on pages 22 and 32.

Students now read the **Study Skill** on page 52.

Read the instructions and look at the notes with the class. Deal with any difficulties, and tell students to copy the note diagram into their notebooks.

Students read the article again and complete the notes individually.

Check answers and write a possible version of the notes on the board with the class. **⟳ 5**

6 Read the instructions with the class and make sure students understand they should use their notes (not the article) to answer the questions.

Check answers with the class. **⟳ 6a**

EXTENSION ACTIVITY

Ask students to look back at the text *How do you read?* in Unit 1 (page 5). Write the title on the board. Ask them to read the second and third paragraphs of the text and to make linear notes. Check the students' notes. Write the following on the board as a possible answer. **⟳ 6b**

READING Answer key pp52–53

⟳ 2

1a 2b 3d 4d

⟳ 3

a4 b5 c3 d1 e2

⟳ 4

a do workouts
b mix with other people
c good
d stay away from
e good for you
f helps the brain work better

⟳ 5

Possible answer

Socially active	– join social clubs and groups
	– travel to other countries to meet new people
	– learn new skills (e.g. skiing)
Brain-healthy diet	– avoid fatty foods/ food with high cholesterol
	– eat vegetables, fruit, fish, nuts
	– some foods (e.g. liver, eggs) improve brainpower
Physical activity	– good flow of blood to the brain
	– encourages new cells
	– but take care not to damage brain

⟳ 6a

Possible answers

1 We can do quizzes or puzzles.
2 We can join social clubs or travel to other countries.
3 It keeps a good flow of blood to the brain and encourages new cells.
4 Fatty food and food with high cholesterol is bad for the brain.
5 Vegetables, fruit, and fish are good for the brain.

⟳ 6b

Possible answer

1 Reading quickly
  a) skimming – to get the general meaning, e.g. from a newspaper
  b) scanning – for a piece of information, e.g telephone number
2 Reading carefully
  a) intensive or study reading, e.g. textbook
  b) learning by heart, e.g. poem

WRITING Notes and summaries pp54–55

AIMS

This section aims to raise students' awareness of the common types of error made by learners of English, and to encourage them to think about the types of error that they are making in their own writing. It also helps students write short summaries of texts, using notes that they have made.

LEAD IN

- Write a sentence on the board with a number of different types of mistake in it. For example,
  – *My brather are a doctor and he working on a hospital in the France.*
- Ask students to find the mistakes and make a note of them.
- Get them to identify the different types of mistake, e.g. spelling mistake, verb form, incorrect preposition.
- Elicit other types of mistake, e.g. capitalization and punctuation. Ask students what types of mistake they often make.

PROCEDURE

1 Students read the **Study Skill**. They then match the mistakes to the sentences. Students check their answers in pairs before you check with the class. **⊶1**

2 Refer students to the picture of Albert Einstein and ask students what they know about him.

Students then read the instructions and correct the mistakes in the paragraph. **⊶2**

3 Read the instructions with the class, then put students into pairs or small groups to discuss the questions. Bring the whole class together to discuss the answers. Note down any common points on the board.

4 Tell students they are going to read a text about sleep. Ask them a few questions about the topic, e.g. *Why is sleep important? How many hours sleep do you usually have? What do you do if you can't sleep?*

Direct the students attention to the text and the notes. Read through the notes briefly with the class.

Students then read the text carefully and complete the notes. Check their notes. Together with the class write a possible answer on the board. **⊶4**

5 Tell students to read the **Study Skill**. Point out that we usually write a summary from notes, not from the original text.

Students then complete the summary in their own words, using their notes. Check the students' summaries and give them a possible answer. **⊶5**

Writing a summary p55

6 Students now look at the notes they made on the brain (page 52). Students write a short summary of the text. **⊶6**

EXTENSION ACTIVITY

Find a short text of interest to students which is at the right language level. Alternatively, ask students to bring their own texts to class. Go through the text quickly and check comprehension. Then ask students to make notes on the text. Check the notes and discuss them with the class. Finally, get the students to use their notes to write a summary.

ADDITIONAL PHOTOCOPIABLE ACTIVITY

Writing 9 Summarizing

WRITING Answer key pp54–55

⊶1

1 c My brother **is** studying …
2 e Bill Gates **began** programming …
3 b Atilla is **a** student at …
4 d How **can we** measure …
5 f We know that exercise **is** good …
6 a I have a lecture **on** Tuesday …

⊶2

~~lives~~ **lived**
~~the~~ **a**
~~were~~ **was**
~~which in 1915 he discovered~~ **which he discovered in 1915**
~~On~~ **In**
Einstein **was** the greatest scientist …

⊶4

Possible answers
1 **Importance of sleep**
  - during sleep: brain repairs itself
                   stores information
  - no sleep: tired; cannot remember;
                   may become ill

2 **What stops sleep?**
  - not relaxed
  - thinking about work/studies
  - late at night: phone calls/emails
                    drinks with caffeine/dinner

3 **What can we do to sleep well?**
  - a comfortable bed
  - a dark, quiet room
  - every night – same routine (book, bath, music, etc)

⊶5

Possible answer
During sleep the brain repairs itself and stores information. If we do not sleep, then the brain becomes tired. We cannot remember things and we may become ill. People sleep badly when they are not relaxed. They are thinking about their work or studies. Late at night they make phone calls, and look at emails. They also have drinks with caffeine or eat dinner. To sleep well, we need a comfortable bed and a dark quiet room. We also need to have the same routine every night, for example read a book, have a bath, listen to music, etc.

⊶6

Possible answer
We know how to keep our bodies healthy, by having a good diet and enough exercise and sleep. But we can also keep our brains healthy. Firstly, we can do exercises for the brain, such as quizzes, puzzles, and maths problems. We can also remain socially active by joining social clubs or travelling to other countries to meet new people. Physical activity is also good for the brain as it helps the flow of blood to the brain and encourages new cells. Finally, we can eat a brain-healthy diet by avoiding fatty foods, eating plenty of vegetables, fruit, fish, and nuts, and also eating foods that are particularly good for the brain such as liver and eggs.

RESEARCH Books p56

AIMS

The aim of this section is to help students to use books effectively. It makes students aware of the different parts of a book. It shows them how they can use these parts to find out if a book is going to be useful for them, if it is up-to-date, information about the author, etc. It also shows them how to locate specific information in the book.

LEAD IN

- Ask students what reference books they use. Ask them how they find information in a reference book, e.g. read the chapter heading, use the index, etc.
- Tell students that they are going to practise using books effectively.

PROCEDURE

1 Tell students to read the **Study Skill**. Check that they have understood anything and explain any vocabulary they don't understand.

 Draw their attention to the example pages a–e. Students match the parts of the book with the pages. ⊙┑1

2 Students answer the questions using the pages. Let students check their answers in pairs. ⊙┑2

3 Students choose a book and answer the questions about their book. Give students time to complete the exercise and then check the answers of some of the students. ⊙┑3

4 Put students into pairs. Students discuss their books with their partners and explain which parts they are going to read, and why they want to read this book.

REVIEW p57

AIMS

The aim of this section is to encourage students to review the content of the unit and also to practise and develop the skills they have learnt.

PROCEDURE

1 Students read the instructions and complete the task. Get students to check their answers in pairs. ⊙┑1

2 Remind students of the text they read about Albert Einstein. Read the instructions with the class and refer students back to the **Study Skill** on page 54.

 Students now match the mistakes in the text to the ones listed in the box. Check answers with the class. ⊙┑2

3 In groups students now correct the mistakes. ⊙┑3

4 Refer students back to the **Study Skill** on page 52. Remind them that it is usually bad style to repeat the same word in a text. Writers rephrase words, and this also helps with understanding.

 Students match the words and phrases. ⊙┑4

5 Students read the instructions and complete the sentences with words from exercise 4 (*beneficial, avoid*, etc). ⊙┑5

6 Read the instructions with the class. Put students into pairs or small groups. Give them some useful language for their poster, for example:

 Instructions: Go …, Make …, Eat …, Drink …, Always …

 Negative instructions: Don't eat …, Don't drink …, Never …

 Students make their posters. Collect the posters and make a class display.

RESEARCH Answer key p56

⊙┑1

a the title page
b the index
c the printing history
d the back cover
e the contents page

⊙┑2

1 Complete Biology
2 W. R. Pickering
3 2000
4 No – By the same author: *Oxford Revision Guides …*
5 In the index
6 70, 81
7 Chapter 2, Nutrition and health
8 School students – it is for GCSE and IGCSE syllabuses

⊙┑3

Students' own answers.

REVIEW Answer key p57

⊙┑1

1 ribs 2 heart 3 lungs 4 spine 5 stomach 6 hair 7 eye 8 ear
9 nose 10 mouth 11 neck 12 head 13 chest 14 arm 15 waist
16 leg 17 foot

⊙┑2

What know we do … (word order)
… brain   We know … (punctuation)
… was the great mathematician … (incorrect article)
sceintist (spelling)
… they could use   brain … (missing word)
einstein (capital letter)
at 1955 (preposition)
… began to studying … (verb tense)
… his brain were … (subject/verb agreement)
However one thing … (punctuation)
… wider   normal (missing word)
this area … (capital letter)

⊙┑3

What <u>do we know</u> about Einstein's brain? We know quite a lot. Because Albert Einstein was <u>a</u> great mathematician and <u>scientist</u>, other scientists wanted to study his brain. He agreed that after his death they could use <u>his</u> brain for research. When <u>Einstein</u> died <u>in</u> 1955 at the age of 76, scientists began to <u>study</u> his brain. They found that his brain <u>was</u> the same as other brains. In fact, its weight was less than the average male brain. However, one thing was unusual. His brain was 15% wider <u>than</u> normal. <u>This</u> area was the part of the brain responsible for mathematical thinking.

⊙┑4

1c 2e 3f 4a 5d 6b

⊙┑5

1 exercise
2 beneficial
3 delicate
4 avoid
5 socialize
6 healthy

READING SKILLS   Using what you know • Using reference to understand a text • Focusing on statistics
WRITING SKILLS   Linking ideas (8), (9), and (10) • Words and phrases (3) • Writing about statistics
VOCABULARY DEVELOPMENT   Words or figures? • Learning a word – synonyms and antonyms

READING   Dangerous diseases of our time   pp58–59

AIMS

This section aims to show students how they can use reference in a text to help their understanding. It also points out the importance of bringing the student's own knowledge about a topic to a text. There is also a focus on statistics and how they are represented in a text and in visuals.

LEAD IN

- Refer students to the title of the unit (*Staying alive*). Ask:
  – *What is this unit about?* (health, good health)
- Ask:
  – *What is good health?*
  – *How can we protect our health?*
- Elicit ideas such as eating well, getting plenty of exercise, sleeping sufficient hours, protecting yourself against accidents (e.g. wearing seat belts in cars), spiritual well-being, spending time with family and friends, etc.
- Introduce briefly the word *disease* and give an example, e.g. *heart disease*.

PROCEDURE

1 Put students into pairs or small groups. Students read the instructions and discuss their answers. Then get the class to compare their lists. ⊶ 1

2 Students answer the questions in their pairs or groups. Check answers and make sure students understand the terms *developed* and *developing*. ⊶ 2

3 Students read the **Study Skill** and the instructions. They discuss the questions in pairs. Do not check answers at this stage.

4 Students read the instructions and the topics. Explain any difficult vocabulary. Then ask students to skim the article quickly and match the paragraphs (1 to 5) with the topics. Check the answers with the class. ⊶ 4

5 Students now read the article and check their answers from exercise 3 in pairs. Check answers with the class. ⊶ 5

6 Remind students of the use of pronouns in a text. Refer them back to the **Study Skill** on page 43. Make sure students understand the terms *refer* and *reference*.

Read the **Study Skill** with the class and make sure students understand everything.

Read the instructions with the class and go through the table with students to make sure they understand what they have to do. Go over the first example with them. Students then complete the table. Check answers with the class. ⊶ 6

7 Students read the **Study Skill** and the instructions.

Look at the three tables with the class and make sure students understand the vocabulary. Students then complete the tables with statistics from the article. ⊶ 7

8 Students choose a country (their own or another) and find the statistics for it. Ask them to display them in tables. Remind them to make a note of the reference source (website, book, encyclopaedia, etc.) that they used.

READING   Answer key   pp58–59

⊶ 1

Possible answers
malaria, HIV/AIDS, cancer, tuberculosis (TB), pneumonia, diarrhoea, measles, diabetes, meningitis

⊶ 2

Possible answers
developed countries: Germany, Japan, United States
developing countries: Zambia, Sri Lanka, Peru

⊶ 4

a 5   b 2   c 3   d 1   e 4

⊶ 5

Possible answers
1 a disease in which the body cannot control the level of sugar in the blood
2 developed countries
3 it will rise
4 poor diet and lack of exercise
5 reduce our weight, avoid foods high in fats and sugars, exercise regularly

⊶ 6

They: the inhabitants
it: life expectancy at birth
They: people in developed countries
which: processed or fast food
which: Germany
Here: The Middle East
it: diabetes

⊶ 7

Table A	Men	Women
Japan	81.4	87.5
Zambia	38.5	38.7

Table B	Deaths per million population
Germany	183.7
Peru	61.3

Table C	2003	2030
Number of people (20–79) with diabetes	194m	366m
Percentage (%) of population	5.1%	6.3%

WRITING Describing statistics pp60–61

AIMS

The main aim of this section is to help students write descriptions of statistics from tables, charts, graphs, etc. It introduces students to some of the language needed and gives them opportunities to practise this skill. It also introduces students to some further ways of linking ideas in sentences and reviews some of the linking words used in earlier units.

LEAD IN

- Ask students to look back at the article on diabetes. Ask:
  – *How does the writer refer the reader to the information in the tables?*
  – *What phrases does he/she use?*
- Give students time to find the language. Get the answers from the class and write the phrases on the board, for example:
  – *Table A shows that …*
  – *We can see from table B that …*
  – *We can also see from the statistics in table C …*
- Also point out to students how dates are referred to in paragraph 4:
  – *In the year 2003 … , By the year 2030 … .*

PROCEDURE

1 Tell students to read the **Study Skill**. Point out that *on the other hand* is similar to *however*. It usually begins a sentence and is followed by a comma. It shows contrast or introduces a new idea.

Students find examples of *on the other hand* in the article on diabetes:
  Paragraph 1 – *On the other hand, in developing countries …*
  Paragraph 3 – *On the other hand, in Peru …*

Direct the students' attention to the instructions and the sentences. Go over the sentences briefly. Students then complete the sentences with suitable contrast clauses. Get some examples from the class. **⊶ 1**

2 Tell students to read the **Study Skill**. Point out that *as a result* has the same meaning as *so*, but it is used at the beginning of a new sentence. Give examples to show the difference, for example:
  – *Kamal worked hard. As a result, he did very well in the exam.*
  – *Kamal worked hard, so he did very well in the exam.*

Students find the example of *As a result* in the article on diabetes:
  Paragraph 2 – *As a result, the percentage of the population …*

Tell students to read the instructions and look through the sentences. They should then complete the sentences with result clauses. Check answers with the class. **⊶ 2**

3 Tell students to read the **Study Skill**. Point out how *also* differs from both *in addition* and *and* in the way it is used.

Give other examples if necessary, e.g.:
  – *Mumbai is a centre for the film industry.* **In addition,** *it is a busy port.*
  – *Mumbai is a centre for the film industry* **and** *it is a busy port.*
  – *Mumbai is a centre for the film industry. It is* **also** *a busy port.*

Point out that *also* comes before the main verb, but after the verb *to be*.

Students find the examples of *also* in the article on diabetes:
  Paragraph 4 – *We can also see from the statistics …*
  Paragraph 5 – *They should also watch …*

Students now read the instructions and complete the exercise. They can check their answers in pairs before you check with the class. **⊶ 3**

4 Refer students to the picture and elicit that it shows a mosquito. Ask students what they know about malaria (what it is, what causes it, which countries have it).

Students should now read the instructions and look at the information about malaria in the table. Ask a few general questions about the table to check comprehension, e.g.:
  – *What does the table show?*
  – *For which year is the data?*
  – *What regions of the world does the table show?*

Students should now answer the five questions about the table. Do the first question with the class as an example. Let students complete the exercise and check the answers. **⊶ 4**

WRITING Answer key pp60–61

⊶ 1

Possible answers

1 … is very poor / is one of the poorest countries in the world.
2 … they are excellent courses / they are very popular with the students.
3 … there are many disadvantages / many people dislike them.
4 … some people think it is boring / it can cause damage to the knees.

⊶ 2

Possible answers

1 … the total population is falling / there are not enough people to fill the jobs.
2 … many people have stopped smoking / the number of smokers is falling in some countries.
3 … he/she hopes to be a translator / he/she likes travelling to different countries.
4 … many people go there for holidays / it is very popular with tourists.

⊶ 3

1 b Fast food contains a lot of fat. It also has a lot of salt and sugar.
2 f Diabetes is very common in European countries. There are also many people with diabetes in Africa and the Middle East.
3 c Sam runs for five kilometres every morning before college. He also goes to the gym twice a week.
4 a A degree in medicine is expensive because it takes many years. It can also be a very difficult subject for students.
5 e Elena would like to have her own company one day. Her sister also wants to go into business.
6 d Henry has high blood pressure. His level of cholesterol is also very high.

⊶ 4

1 Africa
2 Europe
3 59,000
4 4.6%
5 1,272,000

5 Read the **Study Skill** with the class and make sure students understand all the language.

Students now read the instructions and the words in the box.

Ask students to complete the paragraph, using the words and figures in the box. Check answers with the class. 🔑 **5**

Writing about statistics p61

6 Read the instructions and go through the table with the class. Tell students to use the language from the **Study Skill** on words and phrases in their paragraph. 🔑 **6**

ADDITIONAL PHOTOCOPIABLE ACTIVITY

Writing 10 Describing statistics

VOCABULARY DEVELOPMENT Numbers in texts p62

AIMS

This section aims to show students how numbers are written in a text, when we use figures and when we use words. It also teaches students to expand their vocabulary by learning the antonyms and synonyms of new words.

LEAD IN

- Review the pronunciation of cardinal and ordinal numbers, fractions, decimals, and percentages. Start by writing several different numbers on the board, for example:

  2,890,000   67.56% 23rd 0.025
  $^2/_3$ 37 6,589   48% 16th

- Demonstrate how these numbers are read aloud. In particular, explain how decimals are read, e.g. *sixty-seven point five six* (and not sixty-seven point fifty-six).

- Point to numbers on the board and ask students to read them out.

PROCEDURE

1 Students read the instructions and underline the numbers. Check the answers. Then, without looking at the **Study Skill**, give students time to think about possible rules for when to use figures, and when to use words. Listen to suggestions from the class. 🔑 **1a**

Students now read the **Study Skill** and complete the rules. Check the answers with the class. Point out that these are not fixed rules, but descriptions of general use. 🔑 **1b**

2 Students correct the sentences, using the rules in the **Study Skill**. Let students check their answers in pairs before you check with the class. 🔑 **2**

EXTENSION ACTIVITY

Ask each student to write a list of ten numbers in figures. Make sure they include large numbers, fractions, decimals, ordinal numbers, and percentages.

In pairs ask students to dictate their lists of numbers to their partners. They should check their answers with the partner. Deal with any difficulties with the class.

Using antonyms and synonyms p62

3 Read the **Study Skill** with the class and make sure students understand the terms *synonym* and *antonym*. Point out that dictionaries often give antonyms and synonyms of words. Get students to check the words *wealthy* and *rich* in their dictionaries to see if their dictionary lists synonyms and antonyms.

Students now read the instructions. They should complete the sentences with suitable antonyms, using dictionaries to help them. 🔑 **3**

4 Remind students that it is not good style to repeat words in a text. Point out that synonyms help us to avoid repetition. Students complete the exercise, using their dictionaries to help them. Check answers with the class. 🔑 **4**

🔑 **5**

1 shows
2 see
3 one million
4 89.3%
5 number
6 65,000
7 5.1%
8 was
9 4.6%
10 no

🔑 **6**

Students' own answers, but the text in exercise 5 is a model.

VOCABULARY DEVELOPMENT Answer key p62

🔑 **1a**

1 A hundred and fifty-three
2 153
3 six
4 450
5 first
6 3rd
7 12
8 6.5

🔑 **1b**

a words
b words
c figures
d words
e figures

🔑 **2**

1 2,560
2 four
3 Two hundred and forty five
4 second
5 15.5%

🔑 **3**

1 clean
2 decrease/fall
3 low
4 arrive
5 easy
6 failure

🔑 **4**

Possible answers
1 quick
2 worried/afraid of
3 boring
4 perfect
5 phone/call
6 buy

REVIEW p63

AIMS

The aim of this section is to encourage students to review the content of the unit and also to practise and develop the skills they have learnt.

PROCEDURE

1 Tell students to look back through the unit to find words to complete the table. Students can also use their dictionaries to help them. 🔑 1

2 Students read the instructions and complete the sentences with nouns from the table in exercise 1. 🔑 2

3 Refer students back to the **Study Skill** on prefixes (page 44) and the one on antonyms and synonyms (page 62).

Point out to students that we form some antonyms by adding a negative prefix. Students complete the exercise. 🔑 3

Spelling (4) *-ing* forms p63

4 Read the RULES box with the class and make sure that students understand everything. Students should then complete the table with words from the unit and other verbs they know. 🔑 4

5 Remind students of exercise 6 in the Reading section on page 58.

Tell students to read the paragraph and to study the bar chart. Check that they understand the difference between births and deaths in the chart. Point out the completed example. Students then complete the exercise. 🔑 5

REVIEW Answer key p63

🔑 1

verb	noun
to be born	a birth
to live	a life
to die	a death
to increase	an increase
to rise	a rise
to decrease	a decrease
to fall	a fall

🔑 2

1 life
2 death
3 birth
4 increase
5 decrease/fall

🔑 3

1 unhealthy
2 inexpensive
3 impersonal
4 disapprove
5 illegal
6 uninteresting
7 impossible
8 disorganized

🔑 4

Possible answers

verb + *-ing*	*-e* + *-ing*	double consonant + *-ing*
developing	rising	jogging
growing	changing	swimming
doing	becoming	travelling
falling	increasing	
	decreasing	

🔑 5

Here:	Africa
It:	the birth rate
which:	the death rate
where:	Europe
here:	Europe
It:	the death rate
They:	the countries of Asia

Writing 1 Punctuation

1 Read the first part of this student's description. Write out the text again on lined paper, adding capital letters where necessary.

> my name is abdullah and i am from riyadh. riyadh is the capital city of saudi arabia. i am studying engineering at king saud university. in the future i hope to go to london or oxford to study for a master's degree. my first language is arabic and i am learning english. i can speak english quite well but i think writing is much more difficult.

Example: My name is Abdullah and …

2 Read the second part of his description. Divide it into four sentences by putting in full stops. Remember to check that there is a capital letter at the beginning of each sentence.

> I am 19 years old and I am single I live at home with my parents and my two younger brothers we live in a large flat in the city centre my older sister is married and she lives in Jeddah.

Example: I am 19 years old …

3 Read the last part of his description. Join up the 10 short sentences to make 4 longer sentences. Use *and* or *but*.

> I like sports. I play football. In my free time I also like playing computer games. I don't have much free time now. I like driving. I don't have my own car. I often spend my holidays in Jeddah. I stay with my sister. I like going to the beach. Sometimes it is too hot to go out.

Example: I like sports and I play football.

4 Rewrite the complete description on lined paper. Instead of *I* and *we* use *he, his* and *they*. Make the necessary changes to the Present Simple verbs.

Example: His name is Abdullah and he is from …

Writing 2 Sequencing

1 Read about this student's habits and routines for a healthy life. Complete the text with the words in the box.

next	then	finally	after x 2	later	first

Matthias is 19 years old and lives in Amsterdam. He believes that it is important to lead a healthy life, so he has a daily routine. **(1)** _____ he gets up at the same time every day, at 7 o'clock. **(2)** _____ he eats a healthy breakfast of cereal and fruit. **(3)** _____ that he cycles to university. His university is five kilometres from his home. At lunch time he goes to the university canteen and makes sure that he chooses nutritious dishes which include fresh vegetables or salad. **(4)** _____ his afternoon classes he has a fruit snack. **(5)** _____ he goes to the gym for one hour. Twice a week he plays football instead of going to the gym. **(6)** _____, in the evening, he has a cooked meal made with fresh ingredients. Sometimes he has a lot of homework, but he always make sure that he has time to relax with his family. **(7)** _____, he usually goes to bed at about 11 pm to get 8 hours' sleep.

2 Underline the other expressions which refer to times in the text

Example: <u>at the same time</u> (line 2)

3 Divide the text into three short paragraphs corresponding to the three parts of Matthias's day.

4 Using lined paper, handwrite three paragraphs about your daily routine to try to keep healthy. Use the sequencing words and time expressions from exercises 1 and 2 (100–120 words).

Example: My name is Federica and I live in Milan in Italy. I am a university student. I get up at 7 am every day, and I have a healthy breakfast of fruit and yoghourt.

Writing 3 Pronouns and the words they refer to

1 a Have you ever experienced an earthquake?

b What do you know about earthquakes? Try to answer the questions below.
1 How are earthquakes measured?
2 How dangerous are earthquakes?
3 Why do earthquakes happen?
4 Where have there recently been serious earthquakes?
5 How many earthquakes are there every year?

2 Scan the text quickly to find the answers, using the headings to help you. Note down main points of each section.

> **A   Why do earthquakes happen?**
> Earthquakes happen because the earth is made up of huge pieces of flat rock called tectonic plates. **These** move very slowly, and where they meet is called a fault. When the tectonic plates rub together, the movement forces waves of energy, called tremors, to come to the earth's surface. And **this** is what causes earthquakes.
>
> **B   How are earthquakes measured?**
> Earthquakes are measured on the Richter Scale, which is a system based on the <u>strength</u> and <u>duration</u> of the earthquake. The higher the number on the scale is, the more powerful the earthquake is and the more <u>damage</u> **it** can cause. An earthquake measuring 3 to 5 is considered minor; 5 to 7 is moderate; 7 to 8 is major; and 8 or more is great.
>
> **C   How dangerous are earthquakes?**
> Earthquakes can be very dangerous. They can make buildings fall down and cause <u>landslides</u>, as well as having many other deadly effects. Earthquakes are often followed by <u>aftershocks</u>, and **these** cause more damage to buildings and roads. An earthquake which occurs on the seafloor can push water up and create huge waves called tsunamis. These waves can cause massive <u>devastation</u>. Earthquakes have killed hundreds of thousands of people.
>
> **D   How often do earthquakes happen?**
> There are over a million earthquakes each year in all parts of the world. However, people don't notice most of them because they are so small. For example, although Britain doesn't have a history of severe earthquakes, it has 200 to 250 earthquakes on average a year. About 30 of **those** can be felt.
>
> **E   Where have there recently been serious earthquakes?**
> In recent years, there have been some very big earthquakes. In January 2010 there was a powerful **one** which hit Haiti in the Caribbean. It devastated the country, and between 100,000 and 200,000 people died. Hundreds of buildings were <u>demolished</u> and 1.5 million people were made homeless. Another serious earthquake measuring 7.5 on the Richter scale occurred in May 2008 in the Sichuan region of China. Around 87,000 people were killed, and up to five million homes were destroyed.

3 Read the text again.
a Work out the meaning of the underlined words from the context.
b Identify what part of speech (noun, verb, adjective, adverb) they are.

4 Look at the pronouns in **bold.** What nouns / phrases mentioned before do they refer to?

Example: These (line.2) = tectonic plates

5 Using your notes from exercise 2 and without looking back at the text, write a short description of the main features of earthquakes (80–100 words).

Writing 4 Describing a place

1 Skim the description and answer the questions below. Do not worry about the gaps.

 a What is unusual about these cities in Cappadocia?

 b Where is Cappadocia?

 c Why were the underground cities built?

 d What are they made of?

 e How did the inhabitants make sure invaders could not get in?

> The underground cities of Cappadocia **(1)** *are located* in the centre of Turkey and are a popular tourist attraction. They **(2)** _____ volcanic rock and are thousands of years old. It is believed that they **(3)** _____ because the inhabitants of the region needed to protect themselves from wild animals and harsh winters. These early inhabitants opened deep cavities in the volcanic rock to make cave-like dwellings. Some of these caves **(4)** _____ beautiful paintings on their walls. Later inhabitants made these cavities bigger and created the underground cities **(5)** _____ they could hide from invaders such as the Romans. Houses above the ground **(6)** _____ by tunnels to the underground houses **(7)** _____ people could escape there in times of danger. These underground cities extended down many floors and show remarkable engineering skills. They contained all the rooms, such as kitchens, living rooms, bedrooms, storage rooms and toilet facilities, needed for everyday living. **(8)** _____ also ventilation chimneys and openings for water. The inhabitants made locking stones which could only be opened and closed from inside **(9)** _____ they needed to protect themselves from danger and invaders.

2 Complete the description of the underground cities of Cappadocia in exercise 1, using the expressions in the box.

> | | | | |
> |---|---|---|---|
> | so x 2 | were built | were connected | because |
> | ~~are located~~ | have | are made of | there were |

3 Read the sentences below and add either *so* or *because* to link the ideas logically.

 a The early inhabitants of Cappadocia built caves *because* they needed to protect themselves from wild animals.

 b Later inhabitants built underground cities _____ they could hide from invaders.

 c Invaders couldn't get into the underground cities _____ the locking stones could only be unlocked from inside.

 d Many people visit Cappadocia _____ its underground houses are very unusual.

 e The underground houses of Cappadocia are very unusual _____ many people want to visit them.

4 Write 6–8 sentences about popular places in your country. Use *because* and *so* to explain why people like to visit it (100–120 words).

 Example: Many people visit Rome *because* it has a lot of ancient buildings

Writing 5 Drafting and correcting

1 Look at Fatima Al Shami's letter to Andres Dumont at the International Business Institute.

D

~~dear~~ mr Dumont,

    writing

I am writting to reqest information about your business administration corses at the International business institute. I am 20 years old and I leave in dubai. I left school tow years ago and i werk for a travel company.

I am intrested in doing a part-time course because I want to continue working. please could you tell me if their are any evening classes? i would also like to know who much the business administration courses cost.

I look forward to hearing from you.

yours sinserely,

fatima Al Shami

---

  a Find 10 capitalization mistakes and correct them by adding capital letters.
  b Find 10 spelling mistakes and correct them.

2 Look at Ahmad Al Said's letter to Maria Smit at the International Business Institute.

Dear Ms Smit,

I am <u>write</u> to ask for information about your international business courses. I am especially interested <u>for</u> your marketing courses. My name is Ahmad Al Said and I graduated in Business Studies three years <u>before</u>. At the moment <u>I working</u> as an Assistant Manager for a retail company. However, I would now like to <u>learning</u> more <u>for</u> marketing. Could you please <u>sent</u> me information about your marketing courses? I would also like <u>knowing</u> the starting dates of these courses and the number of examinations.

I <u>am</u> look forward to hearing from you.

Yours <u>sincere</u>,

Ahmad Al Said

---

  a Correct the ten <u>underlined</u> grammar mistakes. Sometimes you will need to add a word.
  b Separate the body of the letter into three logical paragraphs.

3 Now, write your own letter (100–120 words) to the International Business Institute, asking for information about their courses. You want to know:
a) how long the courses last
b) how many examinations there are
c) what qualification you will receive

Remember to divide your letter into paragraphs and to check your letter for spelling, capitalization and grammar.

Writing 6 Internet research task

1 Before you do any research, read the following questions, and try to complete the answers.

   a What is solar energy?
Solar energy is …

   b In what ways can solar energy be used?
Solar energy can be used …

   c What are the advantages of using solar energy?
The advantages of solar energy are …

   d Does your country use solar power?
My country uses solar energy to …

2 Use a dictionary to check the meaning and part of speech of the words in the box. These words are often used to describe solar energy.

to harness	renewable	by-products	pollutants	to derive from
to convert	active	passive	cost-effective	panel

Example: to harness [verb] = to control the energy of something in order to produce power

3 **RESEARCH TASK**

Find 3 websites which explain the facts about solar energy and its uses. Rewrite your answers to exercise 1, adding more information and giving examples.

Example: Solar energy is energy from the sun, and it is created when the power of the sun is harnessed in order to produce energy.

4 Join your sentences together to provide a short paragraph describing solar energy, its uses and advantages, and its uses in your country (100–120 words).

Writing 7 Topic sentences and identifying main ideas

1 Skim the article about chocolate and tick the topics which are covered.

☐ current sales figures   ☐ new plantations   ☐ early history
☐ mass production   ☐ popularity   ☐ religious importance
☐ effects of advertising   ☐ different types of chocolate

2 Match the topic sentences below with the paragraphs.
1 In the 20th century, advertising increased public consumption of chocolate.
2 The origins of chocolate can be traced back more than 1,500 years.
3 Chocolate became a very popular drink in Europe.
4 Chocolate also became an important part of culture and religion in many parts of the world.
5 Until the beginning of the Industrial Revolution, chocolate was largely a handmade product.

A _____ The first people known to have made chocolate are the ancient Maya and Aztec cultures of Mexico and Central America. These people ground the seeds of the cocoa plant and mixed them with seasonings to make a spicy, frothy drink. Later the Spanish conquerors and explorers of South America took chocolate to Europe around 1521.

B _____ In fact, its growing popularity resulted in many European countries establishing cocoa growing colonies in other tropical regions of the world, including Indonesia and Africa. Today, cocoa is still grown in many of these regions. In fact, the Ivory Coast and Ghana are currently the largest cocoa producers and exporters.

C _____ However, new machinery made it possible to create solid chocolate and mass-produce it in enormous quantities much more cheaply. For the first time, most of the general public could afford to buy it.

D _____ As chocolate products became cheaper to make and buy, advertisers introduced marketing campaigns aimed at more people, particularly women and children. Breakfast chocolate became a part of many people's diets. And snacking on chocolate bars was encouraged as a way to maintain energy levels and to improve many other medical conditions.

E _____ For instance, it plays an important role in religious celebrations, such as Easter, in many western countries. In Mexico it is also used to make offerings on the Day of the Dead, a festival of remembrance of loved ones.

* The Industrial Revolution started in the middle of the 18th century

3 **DICTIONARY SKILLS**

Look at the underlined words in the text. First try to work out their meaning from the sentence. Then check in your dictionary.

Example: frothy (adj.) = (used for liquids) with bubbles on the surface, creamy. e.g. a frothy coffee

4 Read the short summary of the article and find and correct six singular-plural grammar mistakes.

> _years_   _was_
> Chocolate was first made into a drink 1,500 year ago in Central America, and it ~~were~~ brought to Europe by the Spanish in the 16th century. They became a very popular drink in Europe, so more plantations were created throughout the world. The African countries of Ivory Coast and Ghana is now the largest producers of chocolate. After the Industrial Revolution chocolate was mass-produced so they became cheaper and more people could afford to buy it. Advertising also encouraged more people to buy it. Chocolate also have religious importance, for example it is used to make Easter eggs. (_100 words_)

5 Write a short article about one of your favourite types of food. (100 words).

Writing 8 Describing similarities and differences

1 Skim the short article on the city of La Paz, and answer the questions:

- Where is La Paz?
- What is special about the location of La Paz?
- Who created the present city?

> La Paz is the administrative capital and the largest city of Bolivia, in South America. It lies at an altitude of around 3,660 metres and is the highest capital in the world.
>
> The city is located on the site of an Inca village. This place was chosen by the Spanish colonists in the sixteenth century because it offered some protection in winter from the wind and cold of the high plateau 430 metres above.
>
> The city is crowded into a long, narrow valley in which the La Paz River flows.
>
> The valley is very narrow, so the city could not be laid out in the usual Spanish grid pattern. Therefore, the Plaza Murillo with the national palace, cathedral, and other buildings, is small. There are only a few broad, long avenues, and the streets rise steeply on either side.
>
> The climate is generally cool, and extreme variations in temperature are common. La Paz is now mainly an agricultural market town, but it also has light manufacturing industries. Its current population is estimated at around 877, 363, and life expectancy is approximately 67 years.

2 Read the information categories in the table below. Then scan the article, and complete the information in the La Paz column in the table.

City	La Paz	Quito
Country	Bolivia	Ecuador
Importance of city		
Altitude		
Location		
Built by		
Built in		
Climate		
Population		
Life expectancy		
Economic activities		

3 Look at the sentences below about Quito, the capital city of Ecuador, another South American country, and complete the Quito column in the table in exercise 2.

- Quito has an altitude of 2,850 metres.
- It was built along a river valley by Spanish conquerors in the 16th century
- The number of people living in Quito is 1,504,991, and the average age at death is 73 years old.
- The economy is based on agriculture and exporting resources
- The climate is cool and like spring

4 Write some sentences comparing La Paz and Quito. Use the information in the table above and use language to express similarity and difference.

5 Write a short article (100–120 words) comparing La Paz and Quito, using your sentences from exercise 4.

Writing 9 Summarizing

1 Read the questions below. Make notes of possible answers.

   a What techniques can I use to improve my memory?

   b What is memory?

   c When should I see my doctor about memory loss?

   d What can I do to improve my memory?

2 Skim the article.

   a Match the questions to the paragraphs.

   b Decide who the article is aimed at.

---

1 _____

Memory is recalling knowledge or past events, and how we collect and store this informations. There is two types of memory. There is short-term memory, which is remembering what is at television that evening. And there is long-term memory, which is remembering information about the friend's life.

2 _____

You should try to get enough sleep and to avoid stress. Without sleep you can't concentrate, and if you are stressed you can't think clearly. Try exercising your brain by learning a language, knitting or playing computer games. A study of 200 people on the U.S.A. aged 70 to 89 find those who had been mentally active in their 50s had considerably better memories. You should also eat healthy. In fact, participants in memory competitions swear by oily fish. Avoid alcohol drinking too.

3 _____

One strategy is to try 'chunking', which mean breaking up information into small bits that are easier to remember. You can chunk a shopping list; example, three fruits (apples, bananas, pears), two meats etc. Other helpful techniques includes rhyming, creating stories, or creating a sentence that uses first letter of each word you want to remember. If you can't remember something, stop trying. Your mind often carries on and will find it for you without your help.

4 _____

You should get medical advice if you fear your memory loss is a symptom to dementia, which is a medical condition that affects mainly old people. Early signs of dementia includes the inability to recall the names of common things, putting items in the wrong place and get lost. Depression, some drugs and too much alcohol can cause also memory problems.

---

3 Read the article again, and look for sixteen common mistakes (prepositions, articles, missing words, word order, verb tenses, subject/verb agreement). There are four mistakes in each paragraph. The first one has been done for you.

4 Write one or two sentences to summarize the main ideas of each paragraph.

5 Write a short summary of the main ideas in the article (80–100 words).

Writing 10 Describing statistics

1 Look at the table showing the statistics for deaths from road traffic injuries in the Middle East. Complete the sentences below:

1 The countries in the table are organized by _size of income_.

2 The table provides information about eleven _____ countries.

3 The number of deaths are per _____ people.

4 The richer countries have a _____ number of deaths than the poorer countries.

5 _____ and _____ have the highest number of deaths, with _____ and _____ deaths per 100,000 people.

6 The next highest countries are _____ with 21, _____ with 19 and _____ with 18 deaths per 100,000 people.

7 In contrast, lower income countries, such as _____ and _____ only have 8 deaths per 100,000 people.

Death rates from road traffic injuries for countries in the Middle East by income

Income and country	Deaths per 100,000 people
Low:	
Yemen	8
Lower middle:	
Egypt	13
Iraq	8
Jordan	15
Syria	10
Upper middle:	
Oman	25
High:	
Bahrain	12
Kuwait	18
Qatar	19
Saudi Arabia	21
United Arab Emirates	29

2 Using the completed sentences from exercise 1 above, write a short description (80–100 words) of the statistics in the table. Check your description for language, spelling and punctuation.

Example: The table shows _____

3 Compare your descriptions and check that you have included all the main points

4 Discuss the following:

a possible reasons for the high death rates in these countries

b what can be done to reduce the number of deaths

Write 2–3 sentences giving possible reasons and 2–3 sentences giving solutions. (80–100 words)

Teacher's Notes – 1, 2

1 Punctuation

AIM
To give students practice in punctuation practice and transfer from Present Simple 1st person singular to 3rd person singular.

PROCEDURE:
1 Photocopy one copy of worksheet per student.
2 Students read instructions, complete the capitalisation task individually and compare their answers in pairs.
3 Students read instructions, complete the task punctuation and capitalisation task individually and compare their answers in pairs.
4 Students read instructions, complete the task by adding *and* or *but* and compare answers in pairs.
5 Students read the instructions and complete the task by changing the 1st person singular to the 3rd person singular. Students will need to be reminded of the 3rd person singular present simple -*s* verb ending.

ANSWERS
1 My name is Abdullah. I am from Riyadh. Riyadh is the capital city of Saudi Arabia. I am studying Engineering at King Saud University. In the future I hope to go to London or Oxford to study for a Master's degree. My first language is Arabic and I am learning English. I can speak English quite well but I think writing is much more difficult.

2 I am 19 years old and I am single. I live at home with my parents and my two younger brothers. We live in a large flat in the city centre. My older sister is married and she lives in Jeddah.

3 I like sports **and** I play football. In my free time I also like playing computer games **but** I don't have much free time now. I like driving **but** I don't have my own car. I often spend my holidays in Jeddah **and** I stay with my sister. I like going to the beach **but** sometimes it is too hot to go out.

4 **His** name is Abdullah. **He is** from Riyadh. Riyadh is the capital city of Saudi Arabia. **He is** studying Engineering at King Saud University. In the future **he** hope**s** to go to London or Oxford to study for a Master's degree. **His** first language is Arabic and **he is** learning English. **He** can speak English quite well but **he** think**s** writing is much more difficult.

He is 19 years old and **he is** single. **He** live**s** at home with **his** parents and **his** two younger brothers. **They** live in a large flat in the city centre. **His** older sister is married and she lives in Jeddah.

He like**s** sports and **he** play**s** football. In **his** free time **he** also like**s** playing computer games but **he doesn't** have much free time now. **He** like**s** driving too but **he doesn't** have **his** own car. **He** often spend**s his** holidays in Jeddah and **he** stay**s** with **his** sister and brother-in-law. **He** like**s** going to the beach but sometimes it is too hot to go out.

2 Sequencing

AIM
To give students practice in using sequencers and Present Simple in a description of daily routines to keep healthy

PROCEDURE
1 Photocopy one copy of worksheet per student.
2 Students read a description of a student's daily routine to keep healthy. Students then complete the gaps using the sequencers in the box. The exercise is done individually, then they compare their answers in pairs. The text also provides a model for students' own writing in exercise 4.
3 Students identify other time expressions. Some of these expressions refer to times of the day, and others refer to frequency.
4 Students read instructions and decide how to divide the text. The teacher can guide them by suggesting that natural divisions could be morning, middle of the day and evening.
5 Students write 3 paragraphs about their own daily routine, using the student text as a model. This exercise also provides the an opportunity to practise handwriting skills. Teachers could remind them of guidelines given in Student's book, Unit 2, ex.1 (p.12).

ANSWERS
1 **Sequence:** (1) First (2) Then (3) After (4) After (5) Next (6) Later (7) Finally
2 **Time:** at the same time / at 7 o'clock / at lunch time / in the evening / at about 11 pm (underlined below) **Frequency:** always /twice a week /sometimes
3 Para 1 up to 'home'; Para 2 from 'At lunchtime' to 'gym'; Para 3 from 'Later, when'.(see text below)

> Matthias is 19 years old and lives in Amsterdam. He believes that it is important to lead a healthy life, so he has a daily routine. **First**, he gets up at the same time every day, at 7 o'clock. **Then** he eats a healthy breakfast of cereal and fruit. **After** that he cycles to university. His university is five kilometres from his home.
>
> At lunch time he goes to the university canteen and makes sure that he chooses nutritious dishes which include fresh vegetables or salad. **After** his afternoon classes he has a fruit snack. **Next** he goes to the gym for one hour. Twice a week he plays football instead of going to the gym.
>
> **Later,** in the evening, he has a cooked meal made with fresh ingredients. Sometimes he has a lot of homework, but he always make sure that he has time to relax with his family. **Finally,** he usually goes to bed at about 11 pm to get 8 hours' sleep.

Teacher's Notes – 3, 4, 5

3 Pronouns and the words they refer to

AIM

To identify words referred to by pronouns; to work out the meaning of subject-specific vocabulary; to write a short description.

PROCEDURE

1 Photocopy one copy of worksheet per student.

2 Make sure the students understand the subject-specific vocabulary: *earthquake, tremor, tectonic plate, Richter scale, aftershock, landslide, tsunami, to rub*

3 Students discuss the questions in pairs / groups. The aim is to activate students' knowledge of the topic in preparation for Ex 2.

4 Students read instructions and scan text individually to find the answers to the questions in exercise 1. The teacher can focus their attention on using the subheadings to help them. Students compare answers.

5 Students work in pairs and try a) to guess the meaning of the underlined words from context, and b) to identify the part of speech of the words.

6 Students read the instructions and in pairs identify the pronoun referents.

7 Students can do this as homework. The aim is to provide writing practice from notes (= an introduction to summarizing), a key academic writing skill

ANSWERS

2 1 by strength and duration / on the Richter Scale; 2 very dangerous, they can cause buildings to fall down, landslides, loss of life, make people homeless, also cause tsunamis; 3 because the Earth is made up of tectonic plates and when they rub against one another there are tremors; 4 Haiti and China; 5 there are over a million earthquakes each year throughout the world.

3 a & b strength *(noun)* = power / force; duration *(noun)* = how long something lasts; damage *(noun)* = harm / destruction; landslides *(noun)* = earth falling; aftershocks *(noun)* = later shaking /tremors; devastation *(noun)* = destruction; demolished *(verb)* = knocked down / destroyed

4 **this** = all the previous sentence; **it** = the earthquake; **these** = aftershocks; **those** = the 200 to 250 earthquakes in Britain; **one** = earthquake

5 **Possible answer**

Earthquakes happen when the Earth's tectonic plates rub against each other and cause tremors. They are measured on the Richter Scale by their strength and how long they last. Earthquakes can be very strong, and they can cause a lot of damage and kill people. They can also cause tsunamis which are very large waves. There are over a million earthquakes every year throughout the world, but many are very small, so people don't feel them. Some of the most recent serious earthquakes happened in Haiti and China.

4 Describing a place

AIM

To find key information about a place, to practise using expressions for describing places, and to write a short description of a place.

PROCEDURE

1 Photocopy one copy of worksheet per student .

2 Students read instructions and skim the text for general understanding (Q. a) and then scan it for specific information (Qs b-e). students work alone then compare in pairs / groups.

3 Students read the words in the box and do the gapfill exercise in pairs. The exercise provides practice in selecting and using key expressions for describing places.

4 Students practise using language for expressing reason and result. They work in pairs and decide when to use *so* or *because*.

5 Students write their own descriptions for homework, using the text as a model, or do as a test in class.

ANSWERS

1 a) they were built underground; b) in central Turkey; c) to protect the inhabitants from invaders; d) volcanic rock; e) they used locking stones

2 (1) are located; (2) are made of; (3) were built; (4) have; (5) so; (6) were connected; (7) so; (8) there were (9) because

3 a) because; b) so; c) because; d) because; e) so

5 Drafting and correcting

AIM

To gain practice in drafting and correcting more formal emails.

The texts provide some clues as regards the correct answers as they often contain the correct form/spellings of words. Students focus on specific errors types, thus making the tasks more manageable.

PROCEDURE

1 Photocopy one copy of worksheet per student.

2 Students do a) first and compare in pairs. They then do b) in pairs.

3 Students do a) individually or in pairs (with a weaker class), then b) individually, using the email in exercise 2 as a model.

4 Students write their own letters as homework or in class, and focus on the need to proof-read carefully.

Teacher's Notes – 6

ANSWERS

1 **a** capitals added are underlined; **b** corrected words in bold.

> Dear Mr Dumont,
>
> I am **writing** to **request** information about your Business Administration **courses** at the International Business Institute. I am 20 years old and I **live** in Dubai. I left school **two** years ago and I **work** for a travel company.
>
> I am **interested** in doing a part-time course because I want to continue working. Please could you tell me if **there** are any evening classes? I would also like to know **how** much the business administration courses cost.
>
> I look forward to hearing from you.
>
> Yours **sincerely,**
>
> Fatima Al Shami

2 **a** text divided into correct paragraphs; **b** corrected words in bold.

> Dear Ms Smit
>
> I am **writing** to ask for information about your international business courses. I am especially interested **in** your marketing courses.
>
> My name is Ahmad Al Said and I graduated in Business Studies three years **ago**. At the moment **I am working** as an Assistant Manager for a retail company. However, I would now like to **learn** more **about** marketing.
>
> Could you please **send** me information about your marketing courses? I would also like **to know** the starting dates of these courses.
>
> **I look** forward to hearing from you.
>
> Yours **sincerely,**
>
> Ahmad Al Said

6 Internet research task

AIM

To research the topic of solar energy on the Internet; to write a short description of solar energy and its uses.

PROCEDURE

1 Photocopy one copy of worksheet per student.

2 Students can work in pairs to share knowledge of the subject and to complete the sentence stems. They can compare their sentences with those of another pair.

3 Students can complete the dictionary work in pairs or individually.

4 **RESEARCH TASK**

Students carry out Internet research in pairs/small groups. They then improve/develop their sentences from exercise 1 individually.

5 Students work individually or in pairs to write a paragraph on the topic. This exercise could be set as homework. As a follow-up, students can read each other's paragraphs.

ANSWERS:

1 **1** Solar energy is energy created by the sun; **2** Solar energy has many uses, such as providing power for homes, buildings, appliances, gadgets; **3** The advantages of solar energy are that it is cheap, clean and renewable. **4** (Depends on students' countries)

2 Answers will vary depending on dictionary used.

to harness (vb) = to direct / use; **renewable** (adj) = that cannot be used up; **by-products** (n) = secondary products / side-effects; **pollutants** (n) = things which damage the environment; **to derive from** (vb+prep) = to come from / originate in; **to convert** (vb) = to change into; **active** (adj) = in a state of action; **passive** (adj) = not active ; **cost-effective** (adj) = economical; **panel** (n)= flat piece of material

3 Websites could include Wikipedia, and factual websites accessed through a Google search for 'solar power' or 'solar energy'.

4 Possible answer (taken from website sources + student's information from own country)

> Solar energy comes from the sun, and it is created when the power of the sun is harnessed in order to produce energy. It includes passive solar energy and active solar energy. Passive solar energy is created for example by the position of windows in a building. On the other hand, active solar energy is created when the heat of the sun is converted into electricity which can be stored in batteries. Solar energy has many uses, such as being used to provide power for technology, homes and industry. It also has many advantages because it is clean, renewable and economical. In my country solar energy is used to provide hot water and heating in homes.

© Oxford University Press 2011 Photocopiable

7 Topic sentences and identifying main ideas

AIM

To identify key points in a text, matching topic sentences to paragraphs, and correct a summary.

PROCEDURE

1 Photocopy one copy of worksheet per student.

2 Students skim the text on chocolate for general comprehension and tick the topics in the box which are mentioned. Students work individually then compare and discuss answers.

3 Students read instructions and look at example, then match the topic sentences to the paragraphs. They work individually then compare answers.

4 Students work in pairs to guess the meaning of the words from the context, and then to look up the words in their dictionaries.

5 Students work in pairs to find and correct the singular-plural errors.

6 This can be set as homework. Students write a short article about a favourite food or drink.

ANSWERS

1 All items in the box should be ticked except 'different types of chocolate' and 'current sales figures'

2 1 D; 2 A; 3 B; 4 E; 5 C

3 Students' own dictionary definitions / translations

4 See corrections in bold

> Chocolate was first made into a drink 1,500 **years** ago in Central America, and it **was** brought to Europe by the Spanish in the 16th century. **It** became a very popular drink in Europe, so more plantations were created throughout the world. The African countries of Ivory Coast and Ghana **are** now the largest producers of chocolate. After the Industrial Revolution chocolate was mass-produced so **it** became cheaper and more people could afford to buy it. Advertising also encouraged more people to buy it. Chocolate also **has** religious importance, for example it is used to make Easter eggs.

5 Student's own articles.

8 Describing similarities and differences

AIM

To identify, select and categorize information; to write a comparison of two cities.

PROCEDURE

1 Photocopy one copy of worksheet per student.

2 Students read the article quickly and answer/discuss the focus questions.

3 Students look at the information required in the table and scan the article to complete the table for La Paz. They compare answers.

4 Students read the sentences about Quito and extract and categorise the information, adding details to the appropriate sections of the table.

5 Students in pairs analyse the information in the table, noting similarities and differences. Check the expressions in the Student's book, Unit 8, (p64), for expressing similarity and difference.

6 Students complete the final writing task as homework. Alternative task: students write a comparison between aspects of La Paz and /or Quito with their own capital city. This exercise provides a basic introduction to compare and contrast language used in IELTS and academic writing tasks.

ANSWERS

1 in Bolivia in South America / it's the highest capital city in the world / the Spanish conquerors

2 & 3 see table below

	La Paz	Quito
Country	Bolivia	Ecuador
Importance of city	Capital	Capital
Altitude	3,660 metres	2,820 metres
Location	River valley	River valley
Built by	The Spanish colonists / conquerors	The Spanish colonists / conquerors
Built in	16th century	16th century
Climate	Cold, windy	Cool, spring-like
Population	877,363	1,504,991
Life expectancy	c. 67	c. 73
Economic activities	Agriculture, light industry	Agriculture, exporting resources

4 Possible sentences to make up a short article.

La Paz and Quito are both capital cities of South American countries.

Both cities were built in the 16th century by Spanish colonists / conquerors.

Both cities are located in valleys.

The economic activities of La Paz and Quito are similar.

La Paz is higher than Quito

The climate in La Paz is colder than in Quito.

Quito has a (much) larger population than La Paz.

The population of Quito is almost twice as large as that of La Paz.

Life expectancy is greater/longer in Quito than in La Paz.

5 Students combine their sentences to form a short article.

9 Summarizing

AIM
To match sub-headings to paragraphs; to write a short summary.

PROCEDURE
1 Photocopy one copy of worksheet per student.
2 Students discuss the questions in small groups as a warm-up to the topic. The aim is to encourage students to anticipate the article's content and language.
3 a Students skim the text to find the answers to questions in exercise 1.
   b The exercise also provides practice in identifying the 'target audience'.
4 Students re-read the text individually to find and correct common mistakes. The activity could be timed, with students then comparing answers in groups.
5 Students work in pairs to decide on main points.
6 This can be can be set as homework. Students write a short summary based on the main points they noted in exercise 4. An example of a summary is provided in the Student's book Unit 7 (p.55).

ANSWERS:
2 a 1 b, 2 d, 3 a, 4 c
   b Older people, 50+ (see paragraph 3)
3 Corrections in **bold**.

> **What is memory?**
> Memory is recalling knowledge or past events, and how we collect and store this **information**. There **are** two types of memory. There is short-term memory, which is remembering what is on television that evening. And there is long-term memory, which is remembering information about a friend's life.
>
> **What can I do to improve my memory?**
> You should try to get enough sleep and to avoid stress. Without sleep you can't concentrate, and if you are stressed you can't think clearly. Try exercising your brain by learning a language, knitting or playing computer games. A study of 200 people in the U.S.A. aged 70 to 89 **found** those who had been mentally active in their 50s had considerably better memories. You should also eat **healthily**. In fact, participants in memory competitions swear by oily fish. Avoid **drinking alcohol** too.
>
> **What techniques can I use to improve my memory?**
> One strategy is to try 'chunking', which **means** breaking up information into small bits that are easier to remember. You can chunk a shopping list; for example, three fruits (apples, bananas, pears), two meats etc. Other helpful techniques **include** rhyming, creating stories, or creating a sentence that uses **the** first letter of each word you want to remember.

> **When should I see my doctor about memory loss?**
> You should get medical advice if you fear your memory loss is a symptom **of** dementia, which is a medical condition that affects mainly old people. Early signs of dementia **include** the inability to recall the names of common things, putting items in the wrong place and **getting** lost. Depression, some drugs and too much alcohol can **also cause** memory problems.

4 & 5 Possible summary

> The writer explains that there are two kinds of memory, short-term memory and long-term memory. There are many ways of improving memory, such as getting enough sleep, eating healthily, avoiding alcohol, learning a language, knitting and playing computer games. It is also useful to chunk information such as lists, and to make rhymes and stories to remember things. According to the author, people should go to their doctor's if they think that they are beginning to suffer from the illness of dementia. (81 words)

10 Describing statistics

AIM
To describe information presented in a table (data transfer). To b come familiar with IELTS Writing Task 1-type writing.

PROCEDURE
1 Photocopy one copy of worksheet per student.
2 Students study the table and complete the sentences individually or in pairs. This exercise provides a step-by-step guide for describing data. The gap fill format means that students have to read and understand the data given in the Table.
3 Students work individually on the next stage in the writing process – assembling the sentences into a paragraph. Students also need to focus attention on proof-reading.
4 Students compare their descriptions in pairs and revise the content of their text.
5 Students in pairs/groups discuss possible reasons for these statistics and make recommendations. This will be required in undergraduate and postgraduate university studies, but is not required for IELTS (hence the separation of this from the writing task in ex 2)
6 Students can read an 'academic' text – this will prepare them for the types of text they will have to deal with on university courses. They can check the text to see if any of their ideas are included.

Teacher's Notes

ANSWERS

1 2 Middle-Eastern; 3 100,000; 4 higher; 5 United Arab Emirates
/ Oman / 29 / 25; 6 Saudi Arabia / Qatar / Kuwait; 7 Yemen /
Iraq

2 Possible answer

> The table shows the death rates from road accidents in 11 Middle
> Eastern countries. It indicates that the countries with the highest
> income have the highest death rates. For example, the United
> Arab Emirates has 29 deaths per 100, 000 people, and Oman has
> 25. Other rich countries, such as Saudi Arabia, Qatar and Kuwait
> also have high death rates (21, 19 and 18 deaths respectively). In
> contrast, countries with lower incomes such as Yemen and Iraq
> only have 8 deaths per 100, 000. (82 words)

N.B If students are preparing for IELTS, they are not expected
to provide possible reasons/interpretations.

4 Possible answers

a The high rate of deaths in richer Middle Eastern countries
could be because: more people have cars / people drive too
fast / the driving laws are not strict enough / the police don't
fine drivers for speeding / some people don't wear seatbelts.

b Laws need to be stricter / speed limits should be lowered /
drivers should be fined more heavily / the police should
have more power / the driving tests should be more difficult
to pass / speed cameras should be introduced / new drivers
should have to drive more slowly / people in cars should be
fined if they don't wear seatbelts.